# THE ZOETROPE BOOK

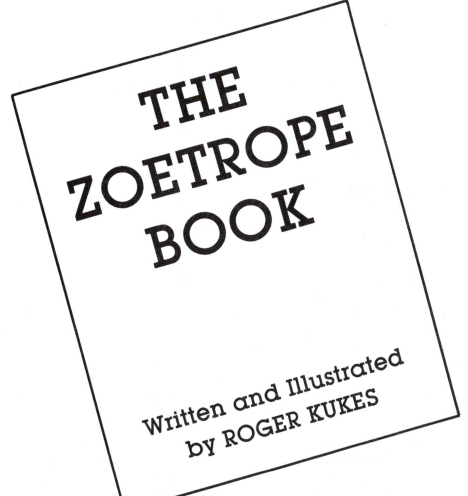

Written and Illustrated
by ROGER KUKES

# KLASSROOM KINETICS

Portland, Oregon

*For my mother Bea,*

*who taught me to love the arts*

*and to believe in myself.*

## Acknowledgments

Heartfelt thanks are due to so many...

To my multi-talented wife, Linnea, for her love and support--and for her skills as editor and designer.  To Susie "Golden Hands" Kobelin, not only for her peerless typing of the entire book, but for her patience, good humor and friendship.  To Jim Blashfield, Judy Mann, Ken O'Connell and Jim Samuels for their unflagging encouragement.  To Kent Snyder for generously making office space and business machines available to me for the book's production.  To Howard Aaron for his enthusiastic Foreword. To Eleanor Kukes for her careful reading of the manuscript.  To Sharon Niemcyzk for information on making durable zoetropes.  To Suzanne Crawford and Maya Kukes for their delightful drawings.

Special thanks to Matthew Lyon and Cindy Stinson-Chennell, and to all the other animators who granted permission to reproduce their wonderful strips.  Alas, some of the strips in the book are not credited.  The makers of these strips are unknown to me.  (The strips were left behind after classes ended, or were given to me unsigned long before I thought of writing The Zoetrope Book).  To these unacknowledged creators, my apologies.  Hopefully, future editions of this book will include their names.

Roger Kukes

Copyright 1985 by Roger Kukes
All rights reserved.
Library of Congress catalog card number: 85-80709
ISBN #0-9622330-0-5
Second Printing August 1989
Cover Design:  Linnea Gilson

Published by: Klassroom Kinetics
              3758 SE Taylor Street
              Portland, Oregon  97214

THE
ZOETROPE,
OR
WHEEL OF LIFE.

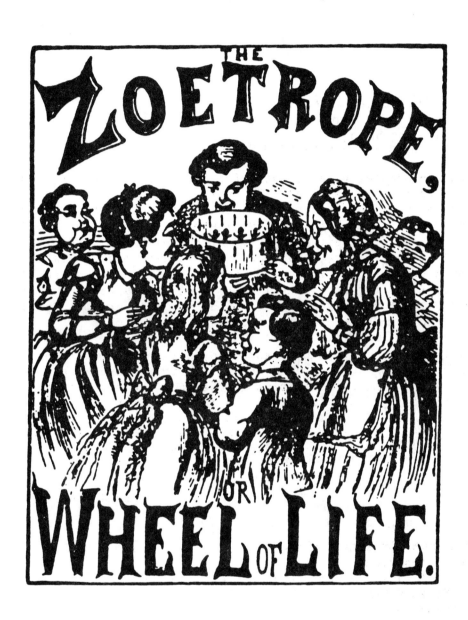

# Contents

Cover Design:    Linnea Gilson

Cover Zoetrope Strips by:    Su Ju Su, Dick Saulsbury, Cindy Stinson-Chennell, Kathy Larsen, Roger Kukes, Ken O'Connell, Betty Bethune, Steve Tackett, Pierre Dunn and Nancy McElroy.

# Foreward

For someone in this age of technological hyperbole to devote himself to one of the most wonderful of Victorian parlor toys, the zoetrope, is now our collective good fortune. Roger Kukes' The Zoetrope Book is more than a new arts resource, it succeeds in inviting our participation. Drawing upon the author's years of experience as a visual artist, independent animator and teacher, the book brings to life the magic of animation through exquisite children's drawings, charming illustrations and carefully thought out directions. The reader is given a bounty of practical information on the art of animation, on different ways to make your own zoetropes, and he provides sample exercises that are a delight to take part in. And to think the excitement the book generates is based upon an optical toy that has been around for more than 100 years!

Animation has been considered the most universal of art forms, transcending language and culture barriers and allowing us to think in purely visual terms. Animation is also a powerful tool for personal expression and learning. Teachers searching for new ways to challenge their students will find The Zoetrope Book to be a tremendous guide, not only for working in the visual and media arts, but across a variety of curriculum areas. Parents will find the book full of activities the whole family can share in. The zoetrope's range is astonishingly wide; I'm not exaggerating when I say that everyone from kindergartners to art professionals will be equally challenged and engaged. I also think, quite unabashedly, the book is fun.

Roger Kukes' love of the zoetrope is always apparent and I'm sure whoever picks up the book will begin zoetroping. So get to it. I know you'll find no better guide.

Howard Aaron
Assistant Director
Northwest Film Study Center
Portland, Oregon

# Introduction

As the 20th Century winds down, I'm reminded of a story my Grandma told me when I was eight. "In 1914 we got our first telephone. My dad called us all the way from Chicago. When I heard his voice, I almost jumped out of my shoes." Now we have cordless phones the size of checkbooks, credit card size radios, cars with built in navigation systems, retractable-roof stadiums, and digitized high definition TVs. How, in the midst of these mind numbing technological advances can the humble zoetrope, a simple optical toy invented during Andrew Jackson's presidency, continue to command our interest?

In my workshops and classes from Seattle to Los Angeles, I've seen this twirling, cardboard projector elicit the same delighted response from young and old alike. Why? Because the illusion of motion the zoetrope delivers is so unexpectedly convincing, and its mechanics are so simple.

No words can adequately describe the experience of watching images come to life in a spinning zoetrope. And watching is only half the fun. Why not becomes a participant yourself--a creator of your own animated pictures? To those who say--"I can't draw a straight line," my response is, "Don't worry." Successful zoetroping depends far more on good ideas and simple problem solving than it does on "artistic talent."

Whether you are eight or 108, the zoetrope offers you a unique opportunity to express your good ideas as colorful and controlled moving pictures. Kids of all ages love the zoetrope because it makes the animation process easy and understandable. Adults enjoy it as an intriguing stimulus to both eye and mind. Teachers--even in the age of the computer--find numerous ways to use the zoetrope for fun, and as a powerful teaching tool (See Section 4 for sample classroom projects).

This book provides you with everything you'll need to start zoetroping: detailed directions on how to make your own inexpensive and durable zoetrope (it takes about an hour to build one); information on creating moving pictures; the different ways to produce strips, and tips on stimulating originality, and strengthening drawing skills.

To begin, all you need is the willingness to try new things, a little time to explore and a few simple tools--all described in the following pages.

Happy Zoetroping!

> Roger Kukes
> Portland, Oregon

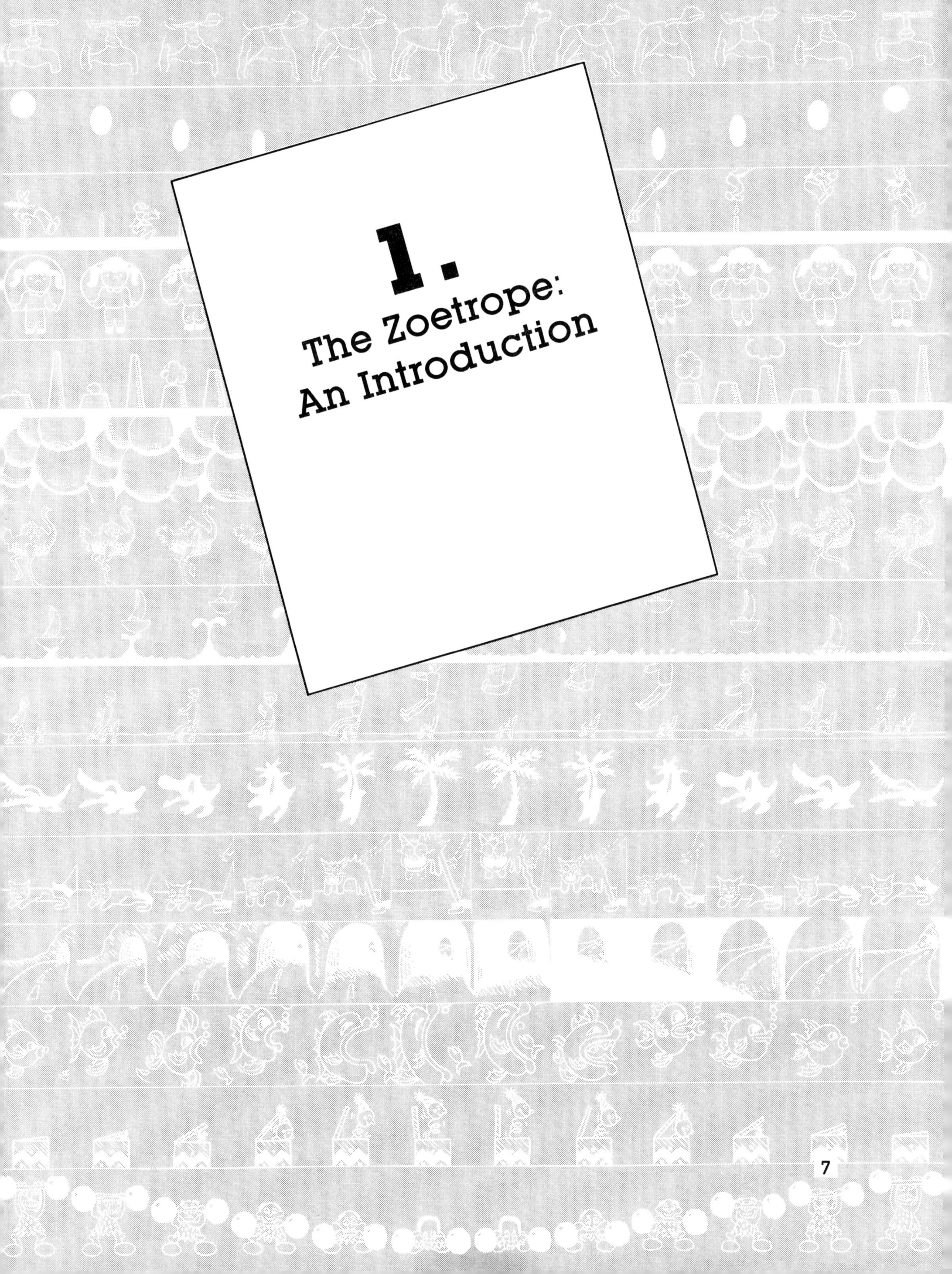

# 1. The Zoetrope: An Introduction

# What is a Zoetrope?

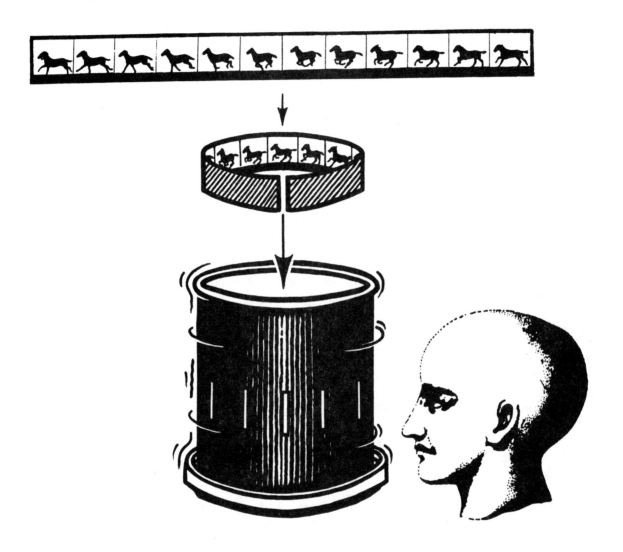

The zoetrope is an ingenious optical toy first built in the early nineteenth century. In it, image strips of every sort--cartoons, abstractions, pure color--come to life as animated pictures.

The zoetrope's mechanics are refreshingly simple. A drum with 12 equally spaced slits is mounted on a turntable or "Lazy Susan". A paper strip containing a series of progressively changing images, like the one above, is coiled around the inside of the drum. The turntable is spun, the viewer looks through the slits and sees--believe it or not--a gracefully galloping horse.

Our version of the zoetrope is made from a 3 gallon ice cream drum. To make your own see page 15 .

# A Brief History

The Zoetrope was one of dozens of optical toys built during the 19th century to display the first moving pictures. Most of these devices had unpronouncable Greek or Latin derived names--like Phenakisticope, Choreutoscope, and Zoopraxiscope. All were based on the principle of persistence of vision first documented in 1820 by Peter Mark Roget. (This principle was one of the most important discoveries leading to the invention of motion pictures).

The first slotted, revolving drum was called a Daedulum. It was built by William George Horner, an English tinkerer, in 1834. Those who saw Horner's jumpy images were aghast and quickly dubbed it--"Wheel of the Devil".

Thirty years later, Pierre Desvignes, a French inventor, refined and marketed a similar device in Paris, calling it "Zoetrope"--or "The Wheel of Life". It became an overnight sensation.

In America, scores of inventors and entrepreneurs experimented with and sold optical devices of every size and shape. One of the most successul was a toy magnate, Milton Bradley, who began selling zoetropes in the late 1860's. His sturdy metal zoetrope--along with a selection of cleverly designed strips depicting energetic woodchoppers, prancing ponies and tireless trapeze artists sold for $2.50.

With the coming of <u>real</u> movies in 1895, the novelty of the optical toys quickly faded. Zoetropes began to gather dust in Victorian attics and museum basements.

Interest in persistence of vision in general and the zoetrope in particular was stimulated by the media surge of the late 1960's. By the mid 70's zoetropes were re-appearing in countless schools, at New Age markets and fairs, in swanky Manhattan art galleries, on college campuses, and in science museums from coast to coast.

In 1979 Portland Oregon's Animation Collective sponsored the First International Zoetrope Strip Making Competition. It attracted hundreds of ingenious entries from the U.S., Canada, England and Japan.

Today's zoetrope "movies" are a far cry from the charming but restrained strips of the late 19th century. They are cartoony, educational, abstract, elegant, personal, kinky, funny, dumb, colorful, and bizarre. Best of all, they're being produced--not only by professional animators and illustrators--but also by kids, film buffs, teachers, athletes, nurses, lawyers, executives--in short, anyone willing to take a few minutes to learn the simple rules of the game.

# Why We See Moving Pictures

The moving pictures we see through the slits of the zoetrope are really an illusion. The illusion of motion is the result of a fascinating physiological phenomenon called "persistence of vision". Here's how it works.

1. A series of still pictures (i.e. frames) are flashed into the eye one at a time through the slits of the spinning zoetrope. The space between the slits acts as a shutter--effectively separating the pictures into individual "stills".

2. Each still (or frame) is seen for about 1/40th of a second-- but the image <u>persists</u> in the visual cortex (the seeing part of the brain) for about 1/10th of a second. This is called <u>persistence of vision</u>.

3. Since images enter the eye at 1/40th of a second, and the eye/brain retains each image for about 1/10th of a second--four times longer--four images can be seen in the brain simultaneously.

4. If the incoming images are part of a coherent, progressively changing series (see horse below), the brain sees the pictures, not as similar stills, but as literally in motion.

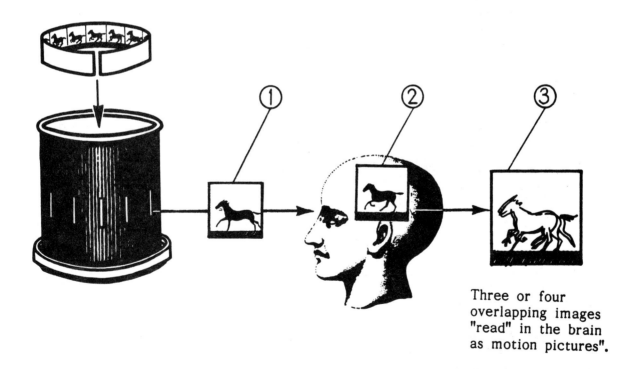

Three or four overlapping images "read" in the brain as motion pictures".

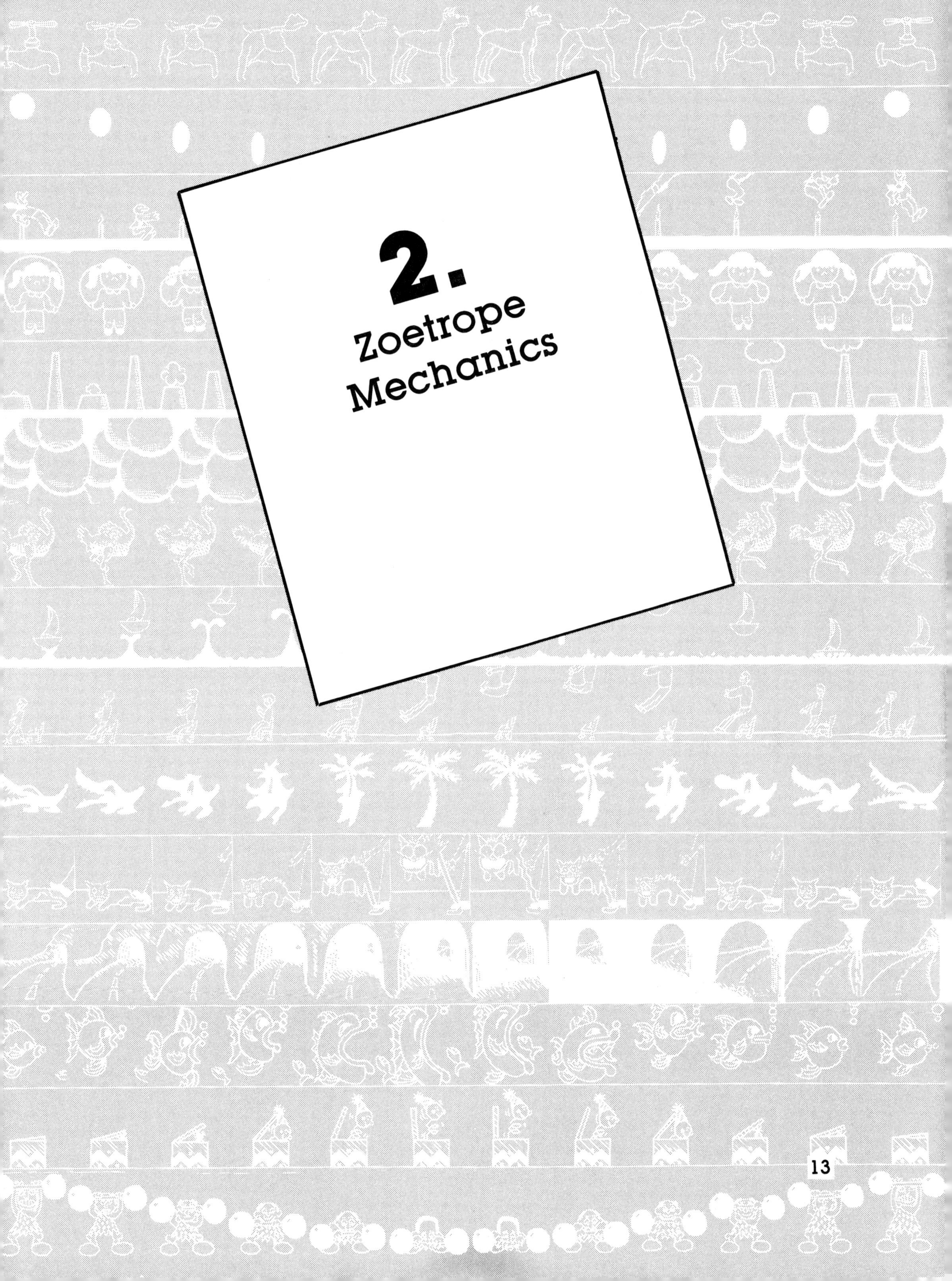

# 2.
# Zoetrope Mechanics

# Making a Zoetrope

## SUPPLIES

Zoetropes For Sale. See page 117.

--Empty 3 gallon cardboard ice cream drum

> Available free--or for a small fee--at many Baskin-Robbins 31 Flavors outlets. Other ice cream makers distribute in the 3 gallon cardboard drum, too--e.g. Carnation, Bresslers, Dreyers...

--X-acto knife with #11 blade

--Pencil, ruler and/or tape measure

--Black paint

> Use Mars or Ivory Black artist's acrylics. They come in 2 oz. tubes. Available at all art supply stores and some big variety outlets. Cheap works as well as expensive.

--Soft bristle brush

--10 1/2" Turntable (made by Rubbermaid)

> A plastic "Lazy Susan" normally used as "cabinet organizer". Find it in houseware section of variety stores

--Barge Cement

> Can be purchased at Birkenstock shoe stores and at selected shoe repair and hardware stores.

## STEP BY STEP INSTRUCTIONS

1. Measure

   Use pencil to draw the measurements directly on the drum as follows:

   a. The distance between the centers of each slit should be slightly less than 2 1/2" on most 3 gallon drums. However, you may have to fiddle around to get the 12 slits to be equidistant (They don't have to be perfect!).

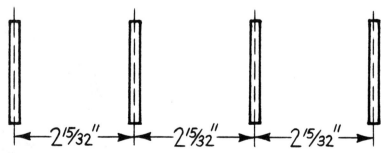

The centers of the slits are 2 15/32" apart on most 3 gallon ice cream drums.

b. Each slit is 1/16" wide and 2" high.

c. The distance between the bottom of the drum and the bottom of each slit is 3".

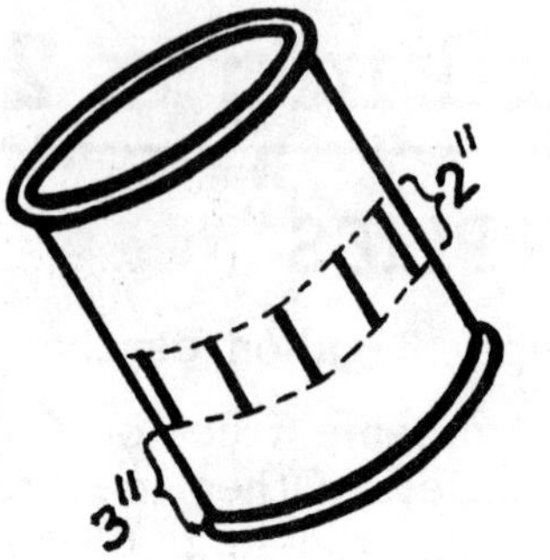
2"
3"

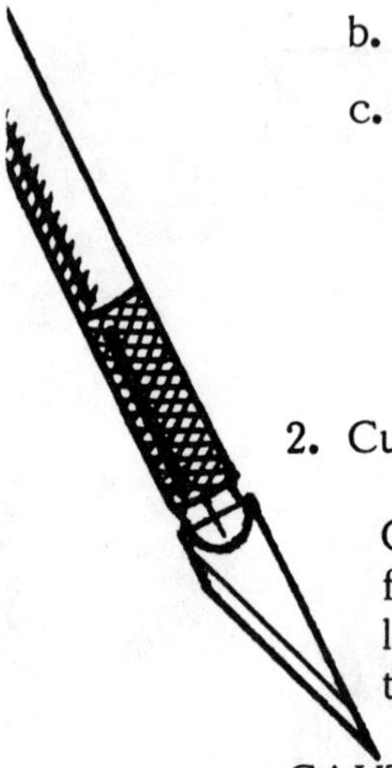

2. Cut

Cut slits carefully with the X-acto knife. The slits don't have to perfectly straight. A few repeated strokes of the blade along the pencil line making a slightly deeper cut each time usually works better than trying to get through the cardboard with one heavy handed cut.

CAUTION: X-ACTO KNIVES ARE EXTREMELY SHARP AND MAY BE HAZARDOUS TO YOUR HEALTH. TREAT WITH THE GREATEST RESPECT.

3. Paint

Thin the paint with water to a milky consistency. A little goes a long way. Apply evenly with a soft bristle brush. Make sure you don't clog slits with paint. Paint the inside and outside of the drum. After the first coat dries, apply a second.

4. Glue

a.

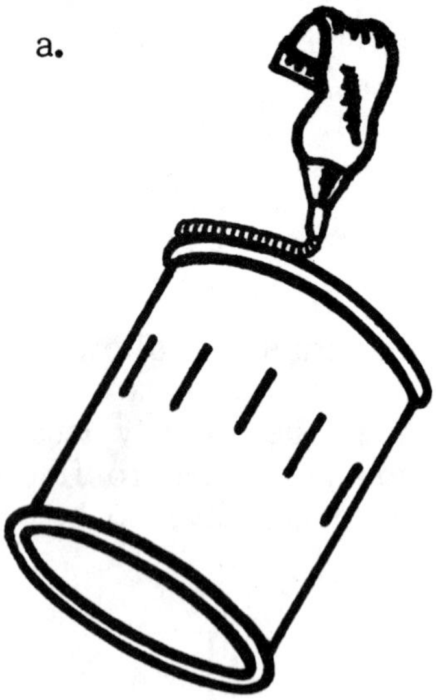

Apply Barge Cement liberally to the bottom metal ring of the drum.

b.

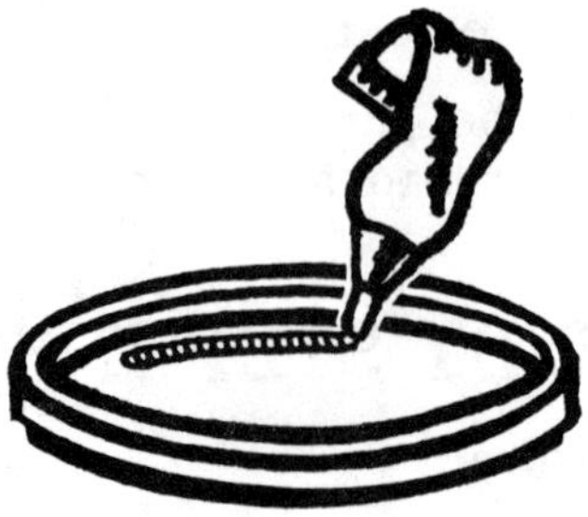

Apply cement liberally to the turntable in a circle exactly the same size as the bottom metal ring of the zoetrope.

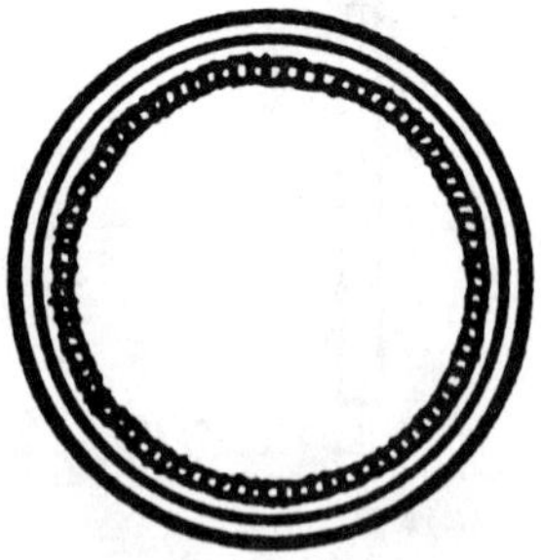

Turntable Topview

c.

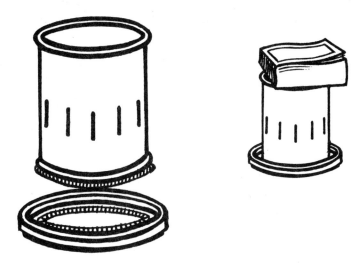

Allow the cement on both the drum and the turntable to set for 10-15 minutes. Then press the drum firmly to the turntable so that the two cement surfaces come into contact. Place a weight (e.g. a telephone book) on the top of the drum to keep constant pressure on the glued surfaces. Let glue dry overnight.

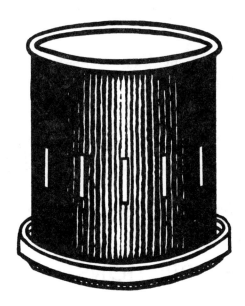

See also p. 98    for instructions on how to build the Short Zoetrope. It's ideal for use in all classrooms--and the preferred zoetrope for kids 14 and under.

# Preparing Strips

## SUPPLIES

--Pencil

--Ruler

A standard 12" ruler is fine if you're working with small (8 1/2" x 11") pieces of paper. A longer (24" or 36") metal ruler works best if your papers are larger.

--Scissors or X-acto knife

--Paper

Just about any kind of paper will do. Heavier papers are the best, especially if strips are going to be handled by young children, or if you're going to be using juicy media--like water color. White's always nice--any color will work. I recommend these:

1. Good old 8 1/2" x 11"

Buy it in packs of 100 sheets (typewriter paper) or in reams (bond or copier paper) at office supply stores.

2. Bristol Vellum

11" x 17". Made by Waussau Papers and others. Find it at paper stores.

3. Butcher Paper

A medium weight paper that comes on large rolls (36" wide) and is sold by the yard. Find it at many art supply stores.

4. Como drawing paper

Very durable. Comes in large (27" x 40") sheets. Art supply stores should have it--or something similar.

## STEP BY STEP INSTRUCTIONS

The following instructions are for 8 1/2" x 11" papers:

1. Measure

Measure and draw lines for three strip pieces A, B, and C.

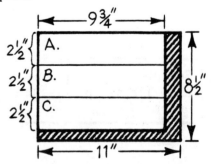

2. Cut

A
B
C

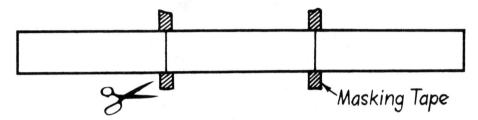

3. Tape

Use masking tape to join the three strip pieces. The tape always goes on the back (non-image area) of the strip.

Masking Tape

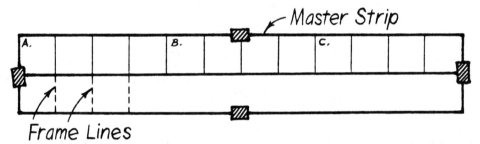

Trim off the excess tape.

4. Draw frame lines

Use the blank "Master" strip (See Sample Strips--p.131) as a guide for drawing your frame lines. Tape down the Master together with your strip and draw the lines with pencil and ruler.

Master Strip
A.
B.
C.
Frame Lines

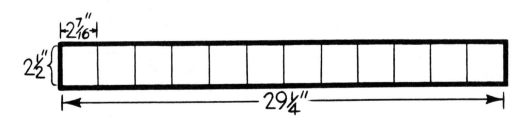

--If you have a light table you can trace the frame lines from the Master on to your strip.

--If you want to avoid drawing the frame lines on each strip, Xerox the Master, cut and tape the strip pieces as described in steps 2 and 3 above.

2 7/16"
2 1/2"
29 1/4"

The 12 frame (12 picture compartment) zoetrope strip above should fit nicely in most 3 gallon cardboard ice cream drum zoetropes. However, slight variations in the inner circumference of drums sometimes occurs, so you may have to adjust the measurements of your strips slightly.

In determining whether strips "fit nicely", make sure that all frames are visible, the drum wall is completely covered, and that no part of the strip overlaps any other part.

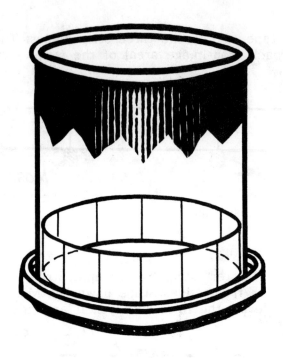

When preparing strips, always make a few extra. Then when a great idea strikes, you'll be ready.

# Viewing Zoetrope Strips

**1.** Place the strip in the zoetrope (See 1 in the diagram below).

Coil the strip around the inside of the drum so that it rides on the drum's bottom and is flat againt the sides. All frames should be visible.

**2.** Tape

If the strip won't stay flat against the inside on its own (most won't), place masking tape "donuts" <u>behind</u> the two ends of the strip (See 2. in the diagram below).

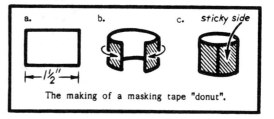

The making of a masking tape "donut".

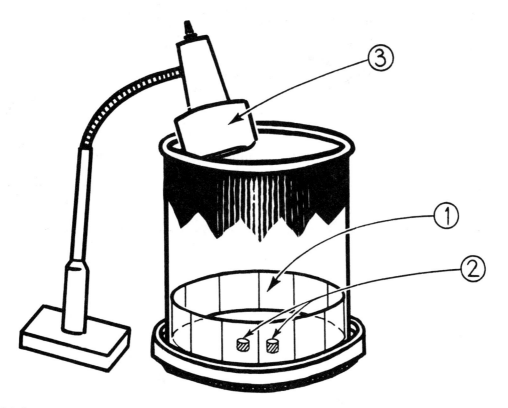

**3.** Light

Zoetrope "movies" are easiest to see when a 100 watt bulb is directed down into the drum. You can use any lamp. I've used swing arm lamps, the Gooseneck variety, handheld reflectors and even flashlights. The goal is to flood the inner drum with a continuous source of light.

## 4. Spin

The zoetrope needs to be in motion for a minimum of 10 seconds in order to really see what's happening. Speed can vary. One revolution per second (more or less) works well for most strips. Any spinning method is OK as long as you keep the drum turning smoothly and continuously.

To keep my zoetrope spinning I deliver a series of short, quick strokes to the base (or lip) of the turntable with my index finger.

## 5. View

Look thru the slits as the zoetrope spins--Voila: Motion Pictures!

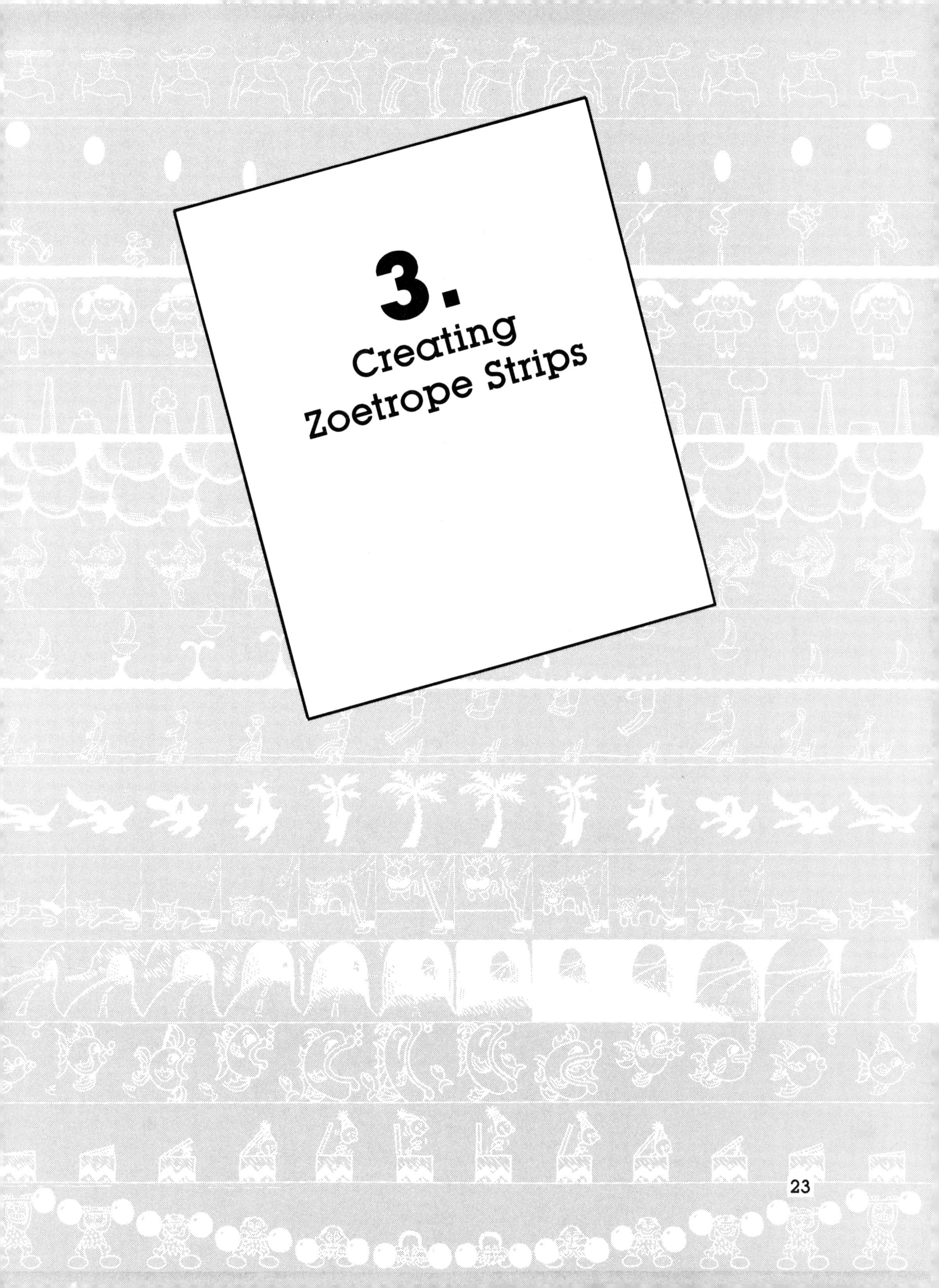

# 3. Creating Zoetrope Strips

# The Big Five

Before we begin creating zoetrope strips there are a few things you need to know. "Zoetroping"--the making of zoetrope motion pictures--involves animation. Doing animation requires an understanding of what I call "The Big Five":

        1 - Ideas

        2 - Images

        3 - Progressive Change

        4 - Motion

        5 - Message

## 1. IDEAS

Every zoetrope strip begins with an idea. Everyone has them--good ideas, original ideas. Coming up with good ideas is primarily a matter of learning to trust <u>your</u> instincts and following <u>your</u> hunches.

People who say, "I don't have any good ideas", are people who either haven't tried or are too self critical. Perhaps both. To begin with, imitating other people's ideas is fine--a great way to learn, but no substitute for the rewards of originality.

To begin zoetroping, you'll need to set aside some time to "Ideate". Quiet time. Hang out the "Do Not Disturb" sign--then go to it.

Over the years I've discovered that my first ideas may not be the best ones--but at least they're a start. Often I use Osborne's brainstorming method:

  --Get into a "hang loose" state of mind (Anything goes!)

  --Generate a series of ideas

      Quick sketches or doodles of how thing might move or change. Remember--"quantity is wanted".

  --Let one idea grow out of another.

  --Suspend all criticism

      Have a little chat with your "internal critic". Tell him (or her) to "take a hike".

## 2. IMAGES

In the zoetrope, any sort of picture or image will work: simple shapes, words, pure color, stick figures, personal signs and symbols, textures of all kinds and, of course, cartoons.

A few tips about images:

--Start simply

--Draw things you're comfortable with (whether abstract designs or realistic drawings)

> Your drawing skills will improve with practice and time. Remember: the emphasis in the zoetrope is on interesting motion--not "pretty pictures" so that takes the pressure off you to be a Leonardo...

--Use media that you're familiar with or have on hand.

> A few #2 pencils, a black Flair pen and any coloring agent (felt tip pens or colored pencils are all you really need).

# 3. PROGRESSIVE CHANGE

Creating convincing and interesting motion in the zoetrope is our number one goal. In order to do that, your subject must be broken down into a series of progressively changing images.

Ask any 6 year old to "read" the images above (i.e. predict the way the drawings will look in motion). S/he will tell you, "It's a bird opening its beak". Clearly, each picture is a graduated step. It's all very logical.

In the five birds above the logical progression has been destroyed. There is no way you can read the images in sequence from left to right as a "bird gradually opening its beak".

Here are a few more examples of changing pictures expressed in graduated steps. Animators call each of these steps increments. Note that changes always occur gradually.

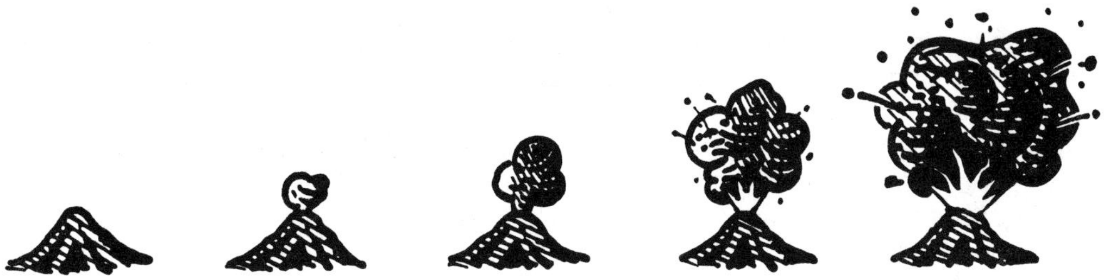

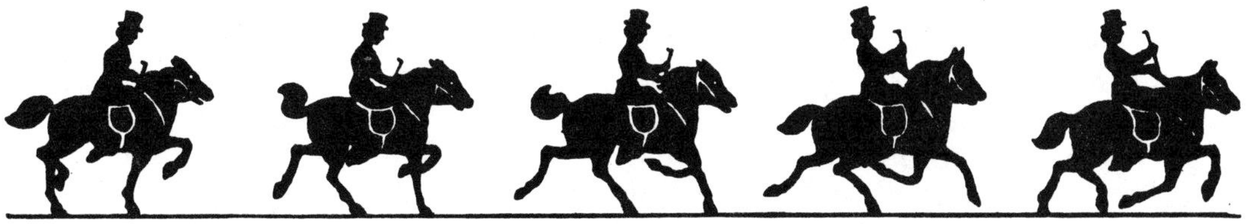

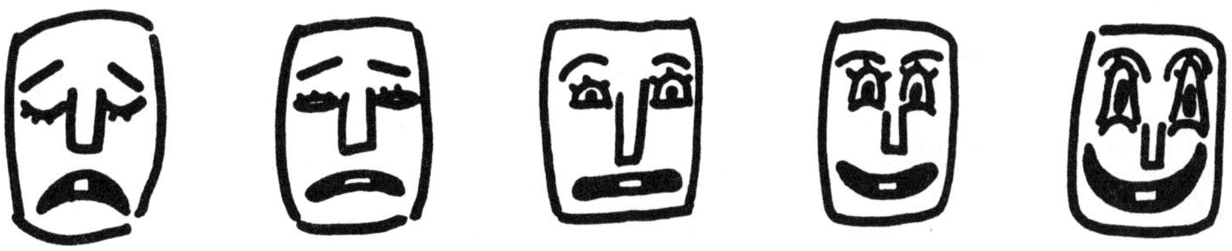

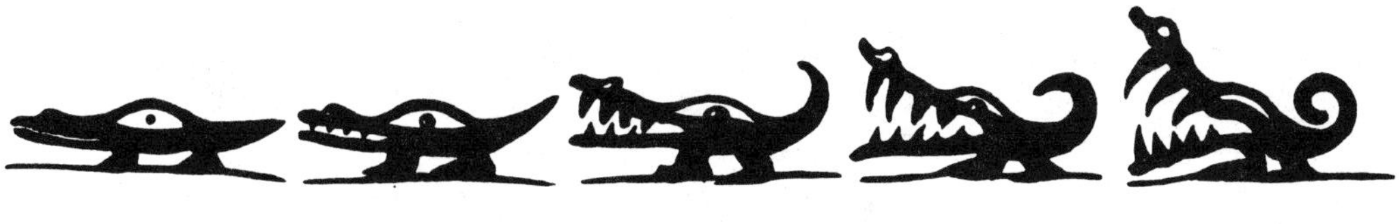

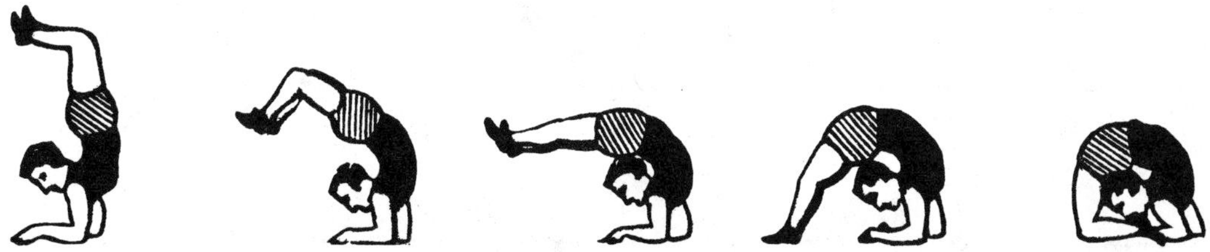

# 4. MOTION

A series of progressively changing pictures displayed in a rotating zoetrope gives us the magic of motion.

The ultimate test for any strip is how does it look in a spinning zoetrope--how engaging is the motion. If your drawing skills aren't the greatest, don't worry. I've worked with hundreds of people (all ages) who were not talented artists but who had two things going for them: good ideas and a feel for motion. They produced <u>wonderful</u> strips.

The biggest challenge to any "zoetroper" will be learning to get images to move just the way you want them to. At times you may want something to move very smoothly, perhaps serenely. Or you might want things to change abruptly. <u>Every</u> type of motion can be displayed in the zoetrope from slow motion to "breakneck".

These factors will influence how quickly or slowly images will appear to move or change in the zoetrope:

--The speed at which the drum rotates

Obviously, the faster it spins, the faster the motion (and vice versa).

--The degree of change occuring from frame to frame

A frame is <u>one</u> of the 12 image squares on the standard zoetrope strip. The greater the change between frames, the faster things will appear to move (or change) in the zoetrope.

As you begin making your own zoetrope strips, keep the following in mind:

Images that change <u>too</u> quickly may not "read" as moving smoothly and fluidly.

Images that change too slowly may be boring.

# 5. MESSAGE

Every zoetrope strip has a message that can be read and described by the viewer. Your idea and your message ought to be pretty much the same. When designing your strip keep in mind that your job is to communicate your idea to others clearly.

Ask a friend to view your finished strips--always <u>in</u> the zoetrope. Don't explain what you wanted to show--Don't say anything. Encourage your friend to tell you exactly what s/he sees. Since no two people see exactly the same way, ask more than one person.

This process will give you valuable feedback. It should also help you improve your work. Best of all, it gives you the chance to share your "moving pictures" with others.

Now that we've discussed "The Big Five" we're ready to begin making zoetrope strips.

# Basic Zoetrope Strips

There are two basic zoetrope strips: The <u>1-12, 6-7</u>, and the <u>Continuous Action Strip</u>. Both are cycles (see below). The 1-12, 6-7 is the simpler of the two. It's the perfect strip for beginning animators to start with.

As we proceed, remember that any kind of imagery you want to use is fine. Often--in my examples--I'll be using simple geometric shapes because it's easier for me to make my points.

## THE 1-12, 6-7 STRIP

The 1-12, 6-7 strip is "cyclical" and has two "holds". Sound complicated? It's not at all. We can make one together in five minutes. Follow these simple directions.

   1. Create the "key" images

      Draw a small circle (or any other simple shape) in the center of frame #1, and the same shape in the middle of frame #12. (No need to use compasses or rulers; shapes need not be perfectly round or precisely centered).

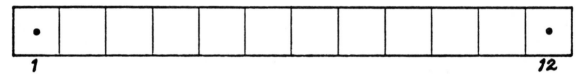

Now draw very large circles that fill but do not go outside the boundaries of frames #6 and #7.

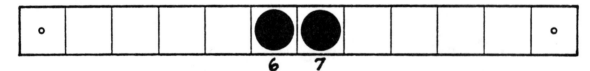

      The circles at frame #'s 1 & 12 and 6 & 7 are called "key" images. A key image is one of the defining phases of a movement. Also called an "extreme", it often comes at the beginning and end of an animated sequence.

   2. Create "inbetweens"

      "Inbetweeens", as the name implies, are the increments between the key images. Simply increase the size of the circles gradually so that frame #2 is slightly larger than #1, and #5 is slightly smaller than #6. Note how guidelines (drawn lightly in pencil) will help you create gradual changes.

Now create inbetweens 8-11.

3. "Read"

"Read" the strip to make sure the circles are changing size correctly. Make any necessary adjustments.

4. Color

Darken (or color) the circles, and erase the guidelines.

5. View

Place the strip in a well lighted zoetrope and spin. Remember to keep the drum in motion for at least 10 seconds. As you view, you should see your circles grow and shrink.

## The Cycle

In addition to creating smooth motion by gradually changing the size of the circles, you've also created a cycle.

A cycle is any action that has no definite beginning or end--but that repeats continuously (e.g. our circle growing and shrinking and growing...). In order to create a cycle, the final frame, #12, must lead smoothly back to the first either by being the same as frame #1, or similar to it.

## Hold

Whenever two or more frames repeat you'll see a brief pause or "hold". The more frames--the longer the hold. If you look closely at our growing-shrinking circle in the zoetrope you should see pauses--both when the circle is at its largest and at its smallest. The more slowly you spin the zoetrope the easier it is to see the holds.

Holds provide the eye with a resting place, emphasize a particular image, and work well when there's going to be a change in scale or direction.

Here are two examples of the 1-12, 6-7 strip. After reading the strips, it should be pretty easy to predict how the strips might look in a spinning zoetrope. Notice that both strips are cyclical, and--as with all 1-12, 6-7 strips--there are two holds.

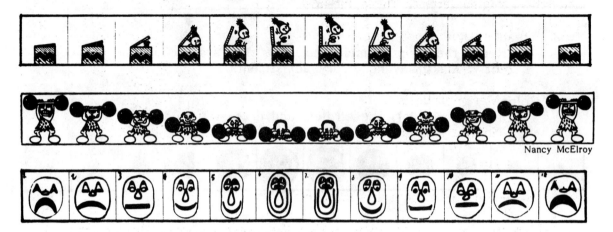

Nancy McElroy

# THE CONTINUOUS ACTION STRIP

The other type of zoetrope strip you should be familiar with is called "The Continuous Action Strip". Like the 1-12, 6-7 Strip, it's cyclical. As you can see in the examples below, frame #12 leads logically back to frame #1, but all the frames are slightly different--including frame #6 and #7. Since all the frames change slightly there are no holds--thus the name, "Continuous Action".

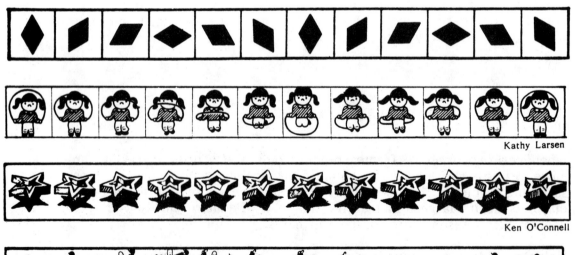

Kathy Larsen

Ken O'Connell

© John Canemaker 1985

# Creating Zoetrope Strips

Now that you're familiar with the two basic strips, the 1-12, 6-7, and Continuous Action, let's explore the different ways to create ever livelier and more original strips. These include:

--Multiple Movements

--Exaggeration

--Metamorphosis

--Spatial Animation

--Lateral Motion

--The Experimental Approach

Each is presented in a separate section. I suggest you read through the sections in order since the information presented is cumulative. Whenever possible, try doing one of the sample strips--or better yet, create a strip of your own design. Doing is always the best teacher and the surest way to test understanding.

One other point. As you begin your work as a zoetroper, keep this in mind: Animation is very forgiving. That is--even though your drawings may not be the greatest, and your changes might be "a little off"--you'll still get surprisingly effective motion pictures.

# MULTIPLE MOVEMENTS

Once you've gotten a single shape to move and cycle smoothly in the zoe-trope, it's only natural--even for little kids--to want to create multiple movements. They are great fun to work out and even more fun to watch.

The challenge of multiple movements isn't to pack the frame with a bunch of arbitrarily moving shapes, but to get <u>all</u> the parts to work together.

"Read" the strip below and describe the three things that will be moving when we view it in the zoetrope.

Now let's see exactly how the strip was designed.

Multiple Movements--A Sample Strip

1. Drew the apples
   After working out my idea, I used the 1-12, 6-7 method (see p.30) to lay out all the apples in light pencil.

2. Drew the worms
   Using the same method (1-12, 6-7) I added the worm, making sure he'd be huge and grinning when the apple was smallest and barely emerging when the apple was biggest.

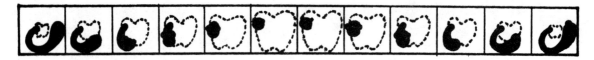

3. Drew the stems
   Finally, I worked out the stems so they'd be tall and skinny at frames #1 and #12 and fat and short at frames #6 and #7.

4. Finalized the strip
   Added dark outline and colored apple (red), worm (gray), stem (brownish green), and background (bright yellow).

Make a quick copy of the strip--and view it yourself.

## Tips on Multiple Movements

1.  Although there definitely is a "point of no return", i.e. a point at which too many elements will confuse or bewilder the eye, it's great fun to see how many things you can get moving and still make sense.

2.  "Idea" Papers

    Before starting work on a strip, try a few different ideas on a piece of unlined 8 1/2" x 11" paper. Some ideas require only a few quick sketches; others demand that all 12 drawings be worked out. Idea papers will help you plan and problem solve. Best of all, they stimulate creativity.

Serene Hill

3.  When designing your strips, create each of the moving parts separately across all 12 frames, just as we did in the sample strip. Do the largest or most important shapes first; then do the secondary ones.

4.  Lay out basic shapes in light pencil. That's the way animators do it. Why? Because changes can be made quickly and easily (animators use their erasers as frequently as they use their leads). View your work in progress in the zoetrope at regular intervals. Don't be surprised if your pencil lines are hard to see. You may have to increase light, darken lines or both.

5.  Distribute moving shapes all around the frame. They'll be much easier to see than a bunch of shapes crammed into one small area.

6.  Try and work out contrasting movements within each frame (e.g. have one element grow while another shrinks, have one element advance while another recedes...). These have greater impact than movements that are similar (or subtle).

7.  Two things will give your images greater presence and clarity:
    --outline shapes with a black line (Flair pens work very well).
    --use contrasting colors: dark against light, and warm (yellow, orange, red) against cool (green, blue, violet).

8. Start off with coloring agents that you're familiar with (felt tip pens, colored pencils, etc.). For more on media see p. 95 .

9. When viewing your work, always make sure the zoetrope is well lighted and that you keep the drum spinning smoothly and continuously <u>for at least 10 seconds</u>. Simple strips will hold your attention for a short time. However, strips where a lot is happening may require extended viewing (30 seconds to a minute or more). Give every strip its due. Remember, viewing is the "pay off" for all your work.

## <u>Multiple Movements</u> -- <u>Examples</u>

"Read" all the things that will be moving in the strips below.

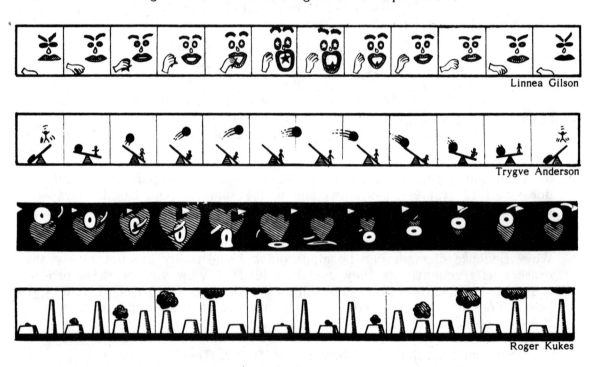

Linnea Gilson

Trygve Anderson

Roger Kukes

36

# EXAGGERATION

Exaggeration means "to overstate" and it's a crucial element in all successful animation. Remember the classic cartoons of the 1930's and 40's? The outrageous antics of Mickey, Donald, Woody and Popeye were all laughably overblown and instantly recognizable. Although your drawings may be much simpler than those of the master animators, learning the fundamentals of <u>exaggeration</u> will help you create moving pictures with ZIP!

Consider these two zoetrope strips:

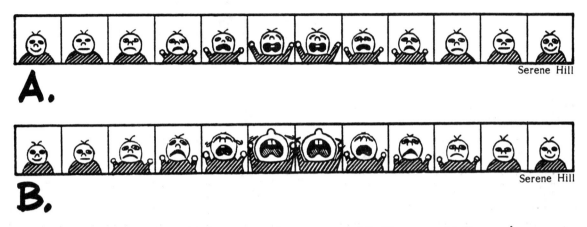

Serene Hill

# A.

Serene Hill

# B.

Which do you think would be more fun to watch? If you said B, you're a winner. In A you can pretty much figure out what's happening: a baby's mood changes from happy to sad. In strip B, the baby doesn't "sort of cry"--he WAILS!!! Notice all the elements that were changed in B: the head and mouth get <u>much</u> bigger, the head tilts back, and tears have been added.

Each of these changes makes a difference. Add them all up and you've got the difference between a strip that barely gets its message across and one that does it with PUNCH!

## <u>Exaggeration -- A Sample Strip</u>

Let's take a look at a strip that pays homage to the old cartoon masters and their penchant for "playful" violence. The idea: a respectable gentleman (you can tell by his suit, tie and expensive hat) is hammered, recovers, is hammered again and again. I call the strip "The Recession". As we proceed, pay special attention to the way the impact of the mallet causes an exaggerated distortion of the head and shoulders.

Roger Kukes

1. Designed the "Keys"

   First I designed the key images, frames #1 and #6; I tried to make them <u>very</u> different.

2. Drew "keys" on the strip

   On a blank zoetrope strip, I drew frame #1 (and #12) and #6 (and #7) as simplified shapes. Using simple shapes helps me stay focused on my primary goal: creating dynamic motion--not "pretty pictures".

3. Worked out the inbetweens -- "rough"

   a. The "rough"

   A "rough" is an animator's pencil draw-ing that is full of searching, tentative lines, yet still succeeds in locating and defining shapes. In the sample "rough" at the right, the flattening of the head is called a "squash". Squash-ing, of course, is a gross exaggeration, yet it's precisely this overstatement that infuses inanimate form with elas-ticity--and elasticity means motion  (the head gets flattened <u>and</u> it will spring back). Notice also that the mallet squashes slightly as a result of hitting the head. The arrows help me keep track of the direction shapes are moving in.

   b. Worked out the largest shapes -- "rough"

   Drew head and shoulders rough in frames #2-#5 and #8-#11. Once again, I tried to keep my shapes simple as I worked out the changes from frame to frame.

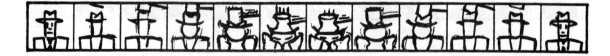

c. Worked out the smaller shapes -- "rough"

> After testing the mallet, head and shoulder shapes in the zoetrope and making the necessary adjustments, I added the smaller shapes (hat, eyes, nose and mouth).

4. "Cleaned up" all frames

> After testing the strip in the zoetrope again, I used my eraser to "clean up", i.e get rid of the inessential lines and shapes. This helped me bring the drawings of man and mallet into sharp focus.

5. Finalized strip

> Added outline and color. (See Tips on Exaggeration, #8).

Tips on Exaggeration

1. An old filmmaker friend of mine used to say, "Any subtlety has a helluva time in the world". Simply put, exaggeration is the opposite of subtlety.

2. The key to exaggerating successfully in the zoetrope involves making frames #1 and #6 dramatically different. (See Exaggeration Examples). Changes from frame to frame can be greater than you might assume and still yield smooth moton. Remember, you have four frames between #1 and #6 to graduate changes--and that's a lot.

3. Initially, present your ideas as simple shapes (most things you'll be drawing can easily be reduced to simple geometric shapes). Once things are moving just the way you want them to, you can go back and make your rectangles into cars, your ovals into faces, etc.

4. Don't forget to use holds (a pause that occurs when two or more frames are repeated). If you use the 1-12, 6-7 method you'll get two holds automatically. Holds not only help your "wildly overstated" images to register with the viewer, they will elongate those moments when nothing really happens (the proverbial "calm before the storm").

5. Opposites lend themselves to zoetroping in general and exaggeration in particular. Think of one of the following sets of opposites as a frame #1 and the other as a frame #6: up/down, happy/sad, big/small, fat/thin, open/closed, deep/shallow, horizontal/vertical. Consider the possibilities for exaggeration!

6. Use speed lines to exaggerate rapid motion. Speed lines are usually a series of parallel lines that follow behind the object and trace its path of motion. The faster the motion of the object the farther apart the increments, and the longer the speed lines.

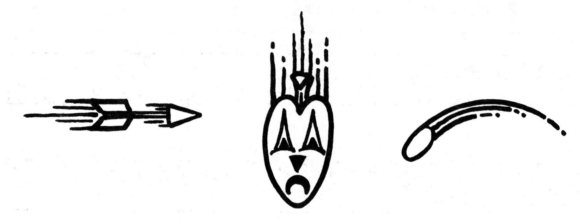

7. Work "rough" and "clean up" after you've tested your images in the zoetrope. If you've done a lot of erasing and the strip is too messy to color, just take a fresh strip and trace the old one.

8. Before coloring your strip, try out a few different color combinations on your "idea" paper. Your goal is to make sure the important elements show up. Use of contrasting colors (light colors against dark and/or warm colors against cool) will help tremendously.

Three thumbnail sketches showing color possibilities for "The Recession".

Exaggeration--Examples

In the examples below, notice the dramatic difference between frame #1 and #6.

Dick Saulsbury

Roger Kukes

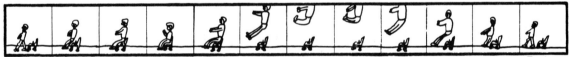

Steve Tackett

# METAMORPHOSIS

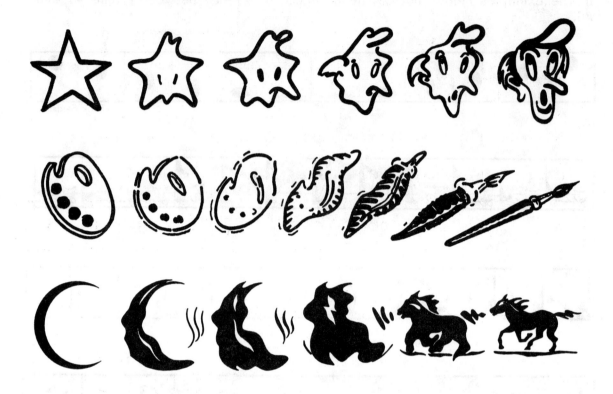

The prospect of changing--let's say--a steam iron into a Great Dane or a crescent moon into a galloping horse is a magician's dream and an everyday occurence for the animator.

Metamorphosis is pretty easy to do with simple shapes, or it can be <u>very</u> challenging. (How about changing a scuba diver into a volcanic erruption?). The beauty of metamorphosing in the zoetrope is that you only have to design six different pictures. In the 1-12, 6-7 arrangement, frames 7-12 are frames 1-6 in reverse order.

Before attempting anything tricky, you may want to try this exercise:

<u>Simple Metamorphosis -- A Sample Strip</u>

1. On a piece of scratch paper, draw or trace the outline of one zoetrope frame.

2. In the center of the frame draw a small circle. Now draw a large diamond that pretty much fills up the frame. These two shapes will be our "key" images, frames 1 & 6. Let's call the drawing with the two "keys" our master drawing.

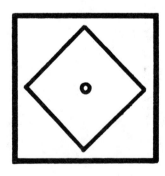

3. On the same piece of paper, work out inbetweens 2-5. Note that the circle not only increases in size, but that the angles of the diamond form gradually.

4. Place a zoetrope strip over your master drawing and trace each shape in the appropriate frame (if you can't see the line clearly, use a light table, or place the master drawing and strip against a bright window).

5. Now trace frames #7-#12 from the master (Frames #1-#6 in reverse order).

6. Color the shapes and view strip in the zoetrope.

## Complex Metamorphosis

Many people like to do complex metamorphosis intuitively: design frame #1 and #6 and go at the task of producing inbetweens with a lot of creative excitement, a sharp pencil and a fat eraser. I have seen some astonishingly deft and fluid strips produced in this way. I tend to be a bit more methodical as I metamorphose. I usually start with a "motion game plan" and work out my inbetweens systematically. Here's how I did the alligator-palm strip. (You'll find a copy that you can view in your own zoetrope on p. 121).

## Complex Metamorphosis: A Sample Strip

1. Designed the two "keys"

   I made them <u>very</u> different in terms of shape, and location in the frame.

Alligator--Frame #1

Palm--Frame #6

## 2. Devised a Motion Game Plan

I started with the two key images and thought about the different ways that the alligator could transform into the palm. I made a series of quick sketches. Finally, I decided I'd rapidly compress the alligator's horizontally oriented body--and as it compressed, I'd begin to form an upwardly thrusting vertical shape that would eventually become the trunk of the palm tree. The palm's leaves could grow out of the 'gator's head almost immediately after the transformation began.

Motion Game Plan

The alligator body compresses (lower arrows) and as the arrows push up, the palm leaves begin to form (upper arrows).

## 3. Created inbetweens 2-5

a. Using a light table and a piece of paper, I drew the alligator (frame #1) and the palm (frame #6) one on top of the other in an area the size of a zoetrope frame. Seeing the two images together made it much easier for me to draw the first inbetween: a shape approximately half way between the two key images.

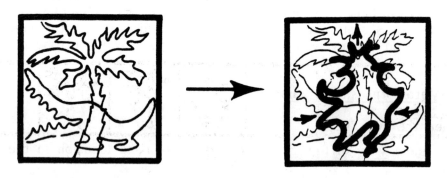

Frame #'s 1 & 6                    Frame #4

The image at the right above was a little closer to palm than to alligator so I called it frame #4. Frame #4 was arrived at through trial and error and quite a bit of erasing. I just kept my game plan in mind. The arrows indicate the direction shapes will be moving in as 'gator changes into palm.

44

Then I traced frames #1, #4 and #6 on to a zoetrope strip:

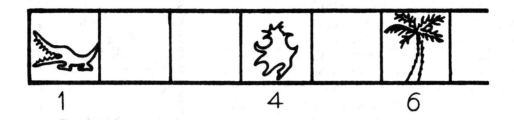

b. Using a light table and a piece of scratch paper, I traced frame #4 and #6 one on top of the other in an area the size of a zoetrope frame. Using these two drawings as references, I drew inbetween #5 which continued the upper thrust of the trunk, and the growth of the palm leaves.

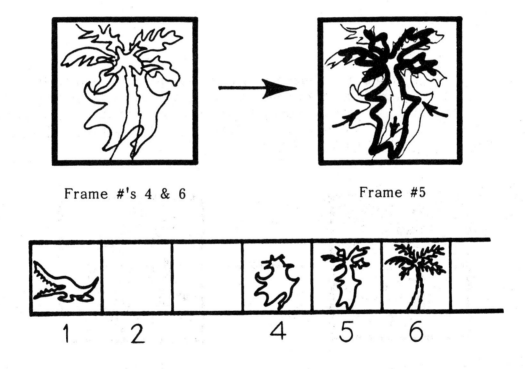

Frame #'s 4 & 6                          Frame #5

c. Using the method just described, I created frames #2 and #3:

--I drew frame #1 and #4 together and designed frame #3.

--I drew frames #1 and #3 together and designed frame #2.

As I designed the above frames, I always kept my motion game plan in mind, worked rough and cleaned up when the shapes looked right.

4. I placed the strip in the zoetrope and viewed frames #1-#6.

 After viewing carefully, adjustments were made to create the smoothest flow of motion between the six frames.

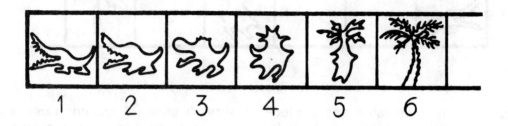

5. Traced frames #7-#12 on to the strip.

 After I was satisfied with the flow of frames #1-#6, I traced these images in reverse order to get frames #7-#12. I viewed the strip with all 12 images in place and made final adjustments.

6. I worked out the secondary movement in all 12 frames.

 The "secondary movement" in this strip was the alligator's eye. I decided to have it rise and stretch (frames #2-#5) and disappear by frame #6. I drew the eye shapes (frames #1-#6) on the strip, viewed them in the zoetrope, and made adjustments; then I drew these images in reverse order (frames #7-#12) so that the eye would be back in its original position at frame #12.

7. Cleaned up all remaining roughs and tested the strip in the zoetrope.

8. Outlined all shapes and filled in with black.

Roger Kukes

Here's the final version of the strip. You'll find a copy you can view in your own zoetrope on p. 121.

## Tips on Metamorphosis

1. Use "holds"

    Since metamorphosis means "to transform", part of your job involves making sure the viewer can see what's changing into what. Use of the 1-12, 6-7 strip will give you two holds and will help the viewer see the crucial key images.

2. When doing simple metamorphosis (or any other kind of zoetroping where a light table isn't available), you might want to use reference lines. Reference lines are lightly drawn pencil lines of any sort (horizontals, verticals, diagonals...) that will help you position shapes accurately from frame to frame. Consistent positioning of shapes means sharper, steadier images when your strips are in motion.

    Different kinds of reference lines can be designed to suit any need--

Sample reference lines

    Here's an entire strip using a simple reference line system.

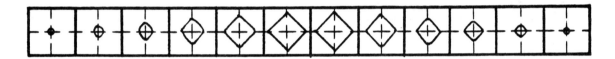

3. When doing complex metamorphosis, devising a motion game plan can be very helpful. The best way to begin is to draw the two key images in the area of one zoetrope frame. Seeing the two images together will begin to suggest possibilities. Then ask yourself this question: "What is the most interesting, dynamic and unexpected way for one thing to change into another?"

4. Work in pencil--work rough and plan on making lots of changes. And remember: changing the shape of one frame will probably mean you'll have to make adjustments in other frames as well.

5. Work out the "big" (or primary) transformations first. Then do the "secondary" ones. Secondary transformations will enrich a strip tremendously.

6. As we saw when doing multiple movements, changes from frame to frame can be greater than you might suppose. Said another way: key images #1 and #6 can be as different as you can make them and you'll still have the frames you'll need to create a smooth and fluid transformation.

7. Color (or texture) can metamorphose in the same way shapes do. Incrementally. For example, let's say frame #1 has a yellow background and frame #7 has a purple background. All you have to do is work your way around the color wheel: frame #2--yellow orange; frame #3--orange; frame #4--red orange; frame #5--red; frame #6--red violet, etc. (See also Color Wheel Zoetroping, p. 78 ).

## Metamorphosis--Examples

Su Ju Su

Roger Kukes

Craig Bartlett

48

# SPATIAL ANIMATION

Pierre Dunn

The world of spatial animation is one in which shapes, characters, and objects don't just move or change in place--they begin to have life in the third dimension. Boxes, trains, birds, planets, arrows, spheres--you name it--can be drawn so they appear to rotate, recede and advance in spaces that can be as shallow as a broom closet or as deep as the night sky.

I won't kid you. Some spatial animation can be very difficult--especially the sort that involves dramatic changes in "point of view" (e.g. moving from a very low to a very high vantage point). Human and animal locomotion can also be tricky. These may require extraordinary drawing skills and practice with both perspective and foreshortening. Not to worry. With limited drawing ability, great things can still be accomplished. You'll need to do two things: first, familiarize yourself with "Different Kinds of Space" (see below), and second, learn to use some of the graphic tricks that will accentuate the three dimensional reading of your moving pictures.

## Different Kinds of Space

In order to illustrate the different kinds of space that are yours to play with, let's use the example of a sphere:

1. Two Dimensional Surface

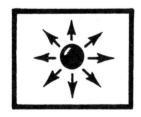

Initially, our sphere is seen on a two dimensional surface. The only motion possible is on one plane. In the wonderful world of animation, prolonged motion on one plane can be very boring.

2. Shallow Space

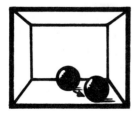

The ball appears to be located in a sort of room. Walls, ceiling, and floor are represented by horizontal, vertical and diagonal lines. Now the sphere can move toward and away from the viewer, but only minimally.

### 3. Medium Space

Now the "back wall" of our room appears to be even further away and there's considerably more room for our sphere to move around in.

### 4. Deep Space

The "sky's the limit". Floor, walls and ceiling are gone. There's unlimited room to move in <u>any</u> direction. In our illustration, as the sphere approaches the viewer, note the gradual increase in its size.

## Accentuating the Third Dimension

Now that you know what your spatial options are, let's take a look at some graphic tricks that will help you create zoetrope strips that have an unmistakable three dimensional reading.

### 1. Size

The farther away an object, the smaller it will appear; and conversely: the closer, the larger. See Illustration <u>Deep Space</u> above.

### 2. Overlapping

One thing positioned in front of another suggests depth.

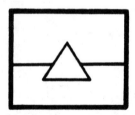

Triangle in front of a horizon line.

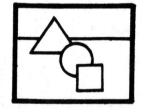

Square in front of a circle in front of a triangle in front of a horizon line.

50

## 3. Motion

Assuming a constant rate of speed, the farther away an object relative to the viewer, the slower it will seem to move--and conversely, the closer an object, the faster it will seem to move.

As a zoetroper, that means if you're showing something advancing, the distance between increments will be smaller when the object is far away, and progressively farther apart as the object approaches.

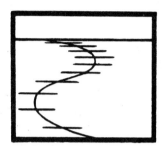

In the diagram at the left, the curved line suggests a path of motion for an approaching object. Notice that the increment lines are farther apart as they near the viewer.

The diagram is called a spacing guide (See p. 54 for more on the making and use of spacing guides)

## 4. Color and Distinctness

Forms in the distance tend to be less intense in color, and less detailed (and vice versa).

## 5. 3 Dimensional Objects

Objects drawn showing sides and tops (or bottoms) suggest depth much more convincingly than objects where only one surface is shown. Note the difference between A and B in the two examples below.

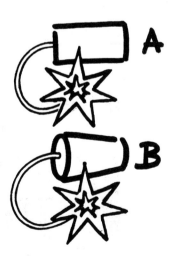

6. Light Sources and Shadows

If the distribution of light and dark in each of your images appears to be the result of a single light source, you'll get objects that look even more 3-D and you'll get shadows. As you can see in the examples below, cast shadows dramatically enhance the three dimensional reading.

Highlight
Reflected light
Cast shadow

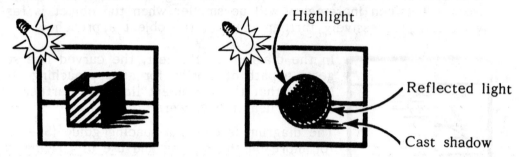

7. Foreshortening

To foreshorten means to present the lines of an object as shorter than they actually are in order to give the illusion of proper relative size--in accordance with the laws of perspective. The use of foreshortening and perspective will enable you to make objects look 3-D even though they're drawn on a flat surface.

Here are a couple of examples.

--Note the compression (or shortening) of the cylinder's horizontal lines as it rotates toward us.

--Notice the foreshortening of the swinger's legs as he approaches. Also note the change in perspective as the underside of the swinger's legs, seat and butt gradually come into view (images 5 and 6).

Matthew Lyon

## Spatial Animation: A Sample Strip

To quickly see the power of the illusion of spatial animation, let's try a simple strip together. Here's the idea: a triangle grows and shrinks while a sphere rotates around it.

1. Create all the triangles using the 1-12, 6-7 method.

   In light pencil, draw the "key" triangles: tall and thin at frame #1 and #12, and short and wide at #6 and #7. Now create inbetweens #2-#5 and #8-#11.

2. Create the rotating sphere

   a. Rotation on a 3-dimensional plane

   The rotation of a sphere on a 2-dimensional plane can be represented by this diagram:

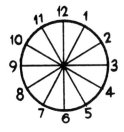

   If we wanted to make a zoetrope strip using the diagram, we'd simply draw a sphere at 12 different positions along the path of the circle (1 per frame). We'd get very smooth motion, and we'd get a cycle.

   Since our goal is to make the rotation look 3-dimensional, the first thing we need to do is to draw the circle as an ellipse.

   An ellipse is the shape that's used to represent a 3-dimensional circle when it's drawn on a 2-dimensional surface.

53

### b. Create a spacing guide

A spacing guide has two purposes: first, it will help you create a smooth path of motion; second, it offers a foolproof way to work out incremental and positional changes.

Our ellipse with 12 increments could easily be used as a spacing guide for the rotating sphere. Draw the ellipse in the appropriate place in a square the size of a frame and you're ready to roll.

Here's what your spacing guide should look like. The ellipse represents the path of motion that the sphere will be traveling.

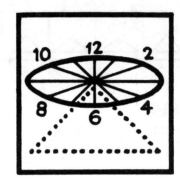

### c. Use the guide

Place frame #1 of the zoetrope strip with triangles over the spacing guide, and using light pencil draw a circle at the "one o'clock" position. In frame #2, use the guide to draw a circle at the "two o'clock" position; frame #3 at the "three o'clock" position, etc.

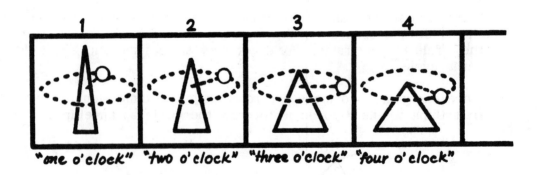

"one o'clock"   "two o'clock"   "three o'clock"   "four o'clock"

When you're finished, you'll have 12 circles, one in each frame at 12 different points around the ellipse.

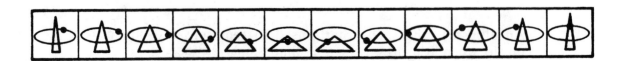

d. Exaggerate the size of the spheres

   We can get a more emphatic three dimensional reading by making the spheres much larger when they appear to be closer to the viewer (frames #4, #5 and #6), and much smaller when they appear to be farthest from the viewer (frames #11, #12 and #1). See diagram below.

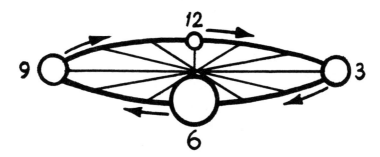

e. Overlap

   After adjusting the size of the spheres, notice that at frame #12 the triangle overlaps the sphere. Erase the circle. This will make it seem like the sphere has gone <u>behind</u> the triangle. Notice that at frames #5 and #6 the sphere will be in <u>front</u> of the triangle.

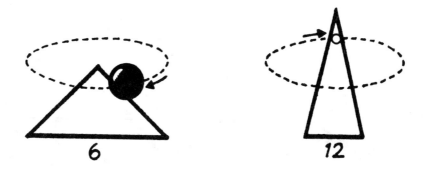

3. "Clean up" and Color

   Color the triangles red and the spheres black. You might want to leave a highlight on each of the spheres. This will accentuate the reading of "roundness". Erase all extraneous pencil lines and view.

## Tips on Spatial Animation

1. The special power of spatial animation derives from this contradiction: we know the zoetrope strip is flat, yet we see lines, colors and shapes moving three dimensionally. Said another way--we can hardly believe our eyes! The more convincing the illusion of motion in space, the more engaging the strip.

2. When you do spatial animation, think of each zoetrope frame, not simply as a flat square, but as a white space having (potentially) unlimited depth.

3. Whenever possible use some of the graphic tricks that will accentuate the three dimensional reading in combination. For example, combine change in size and change in motion and overlapping. And don't forget exaggeration!

4. When doing spatial animation always work in pencil and work "rough". Reduce your drawings to simplified shapes, just as you did in Exaggeration--A Sample Strip (p. 37 ). That way you'll be able to concentrate on priority numero uno: convincing motion.

   Take a look at the three "roughs" below. Though the drawings are quite primitive, almost abstract, you shouldn't have any trouble reading them. The cow can always be made to look more "cow-like" once the motion is working just right.

5. If you're having difficulty visualizing an object moving in space you might want to build a rough (it can be pretty rough) facsimile out of clay (See Media, p. 95 ). Move the clay facsimile incrementally and draw what you see. The same procedure works well for drawing shadows. Create the facsimilie, place a light nearby and draw the shadow that your object casts.

6. If you're going to deal with deep space, you may want to learn a few basic laws of perspective. They are not complicated. All you'll ever need to know can be gathered in an hour or two from "Perspective Drawing" (see Books, p.112).

7. Use spacing guides whenever possible. They will save you valuable time and help you produce smoother animation. When developing your guide, work out the path of motion first. Then, figure out your increments. The increments should be expressed as a series of marks along the path of motion. These marks indicate all the positions your moving object will occupy.

increment marks
path of motion

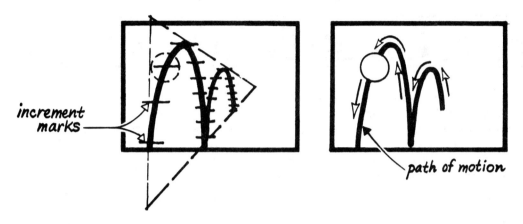

The sample spacing guide above-left could be used to create a bouncing ball (or a hopping frog). Notice the arcs (path of motion) conform to the laws of perspective. Also notice that the increments are farther apart as the object approaches the viewer. In the diagram above-right, I've drawn one phase of the bouncing ball. Notice that the increment mark is located in the center of the object.

Spatial Animation - Examples

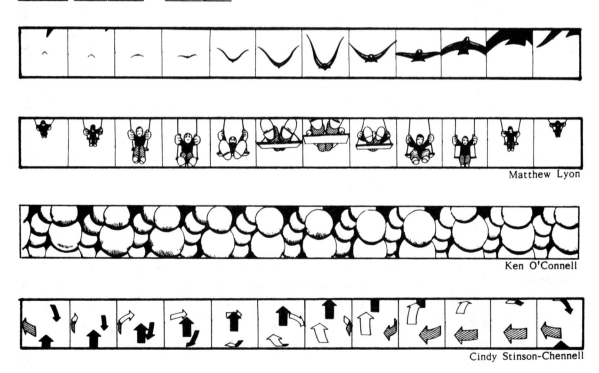

Matthew Lyon

Ken O'Connell

Cindy Stinson-Chennell

# LATERAL MOTION

So far all the different types of motion I've discussed have taken place within the boundaries of the frame. You may have wondered, "Is it possible to move things across frame lines?" The answer is a resounding "YES". Now you'll be able to depict planes, clouds, cars, joggers and bouncing balls moving across your strips in either direction and at different speeds.

Roger Kukes

View the strip above (you'll find a copy on p. 123) and you'll see car and driver tooling past house after house. Look carefully and you'll see that the houses are moving, too--in the opposite direction. The only stationary element in the entire frame is the moon. Notice too, that unlike all the strips we've seen so far, Lateral Motion strips have no frame lines. As you view, remember to keep the zoetrope spinning smoothly for a good 15 seconds. The more complex the strip, the more time you'll need to see everything.

How Lateral Motion Works

Lateral motion occurs when there is a difference between the number of zoetrope slits and the number of drawings. Place a strip having 10 or 11 evenly spaced objects or shapes in a 12 slit zoetrope, spin counterclockwise and you will see your drawings literally move across the strip left to right (10's will move faster than 11's). Place a strip having 13 or 14 equally spaced objects/shapes in a 12 slit zoetrope, spin and watch your drawings parade across the strip in the opposite direction, right to left. Twelve objects/shapes in a 12 slit zoetrope will remain stationary.

Count each of the elements (cars, houses and moons) in the strip above and you'll see why things move (or don't move) the way they do.

Now it's your turn. You can make the simple strip below in just a few minutes.

Lateral Motion: Creating A Sample Strip

1. Tape down the "Lateral Motion Guide" (you'll find your copy on p. 133), together with a blank (no frame lines) zoetrope strip.

Lateral
Motion
Guide

Blank
Strip

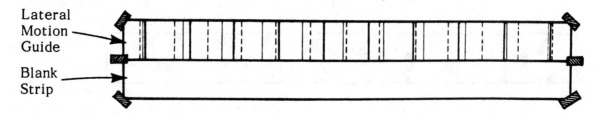

**2.** In the middle of the blank strip, directly below each of the 10 thick lines, draw a small circle. (Draw all shapes in pencil.)

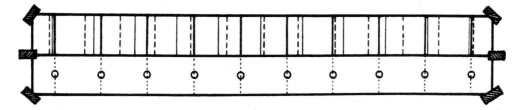

**3.** Directly below each of the 11 broken lines, draw a tall rectangle.

**4.** Directly below each of the 13 narrow, unbroken lines, draw a triangle.

**5.** Notice where shapes overlap one another. Erase lines so that it appears one shape moves in front of or behind another.

**6.** Use contrasting colors to differentiate the three shapes.

**7.** View.

Completed Lateral Motion sample strip: 10 circles, 11 rectangles, 13 triangles.

Just for fun, try adding a "twelve" (12 equally spaced drawings) to the sample strip. Any shape will do. View the strip. Does the addition of the stationary element make the lateral motion of other shapes less or more obvious?

Tips on Lateral Motion Zoetroping

1. Always work in pencil and work rough. Clean up only when you're sure things are moving the way you want them to.

2. The surest way to convey lateral motion is to have your character, object or shape pass something--either a stationary element, a "twelve" (twelve equally spaced drawings), or something else moving in the opposite direction.

3. Because the various guidelines are so close together on the Lateral Motion Guide, it's easy to confuse them. Do each moving element separately--all the 10's, then all the 11's, etc. Since you're working in pencil you can overlap and erase later.

4. The lines on the guide strip suggest the center position for any element you draw--whether small circle or large house.

5. When working abstractly, it doesn't really matter whether shapes are moving Right to Left or L to R. With recognizable objects, it may. Let's say you want to have a speeding car and a galloping horse pass each other. Draw 11 (equally spaced) cars facing L to R, and 13 horses facing R to L. In our 12 slit zoetrope spinning counterclockwise, both will appear to move forward, and past each other.

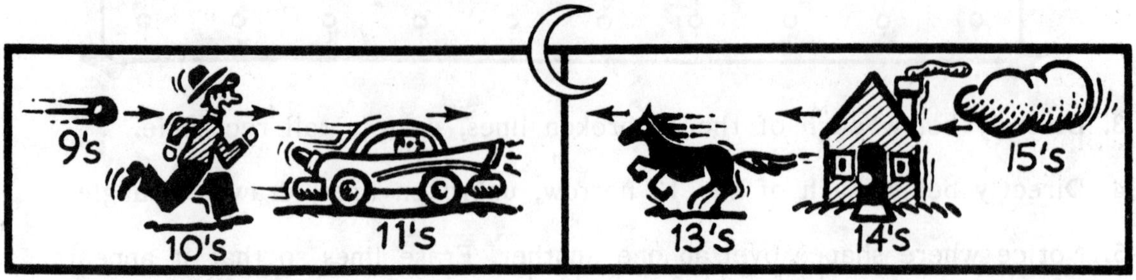
9's
10's
11's
13's
14's
15's

In the diagram above, assuming (as usual) counterclockwise rotation of a 12 frame zoetrope, 9's, 10's and 11's will move →, and 13's, 14's and 15's will move ←. 12 moons will remain stationary.

6. Many lateral motion strips have an unmistakable "deep space" reading. To accentuate a strip's 3-dimensionality, keep the following in mind:

a. dark colors tend to recede and work best with objects that are far away from the viewer.

b. light or bright colors advance and tend to work best with objects that appear to be closer to the viewer.

c. the farther away an object, the slower it will appear to move. (11's and 13's move slowest.)

d. the closer an object, the faster it will appear to move. (9's and 15's move fastest and should be accompanied by speed lines.)

Lateral Motion--Examples

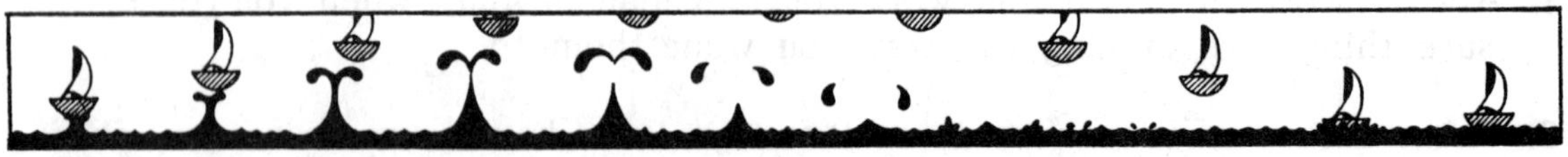

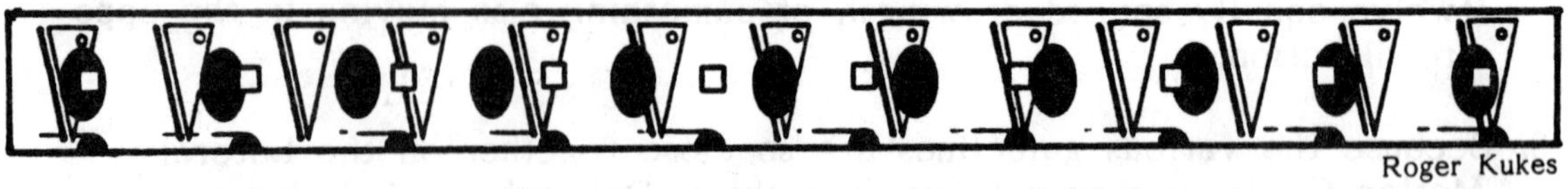

Roger Kukes

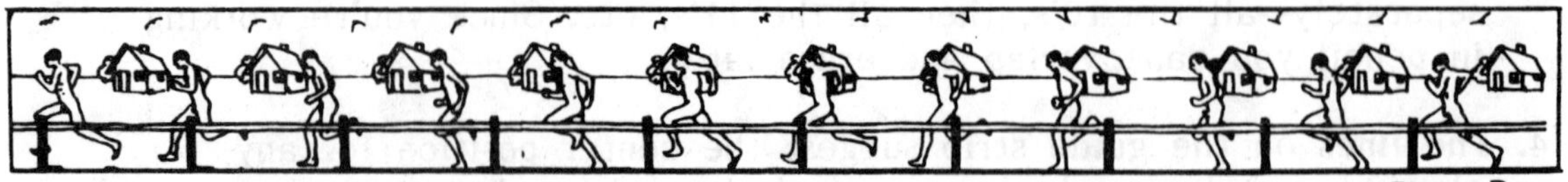

Pierre Dunn

# THE EXPERIMENTAL APPROACH

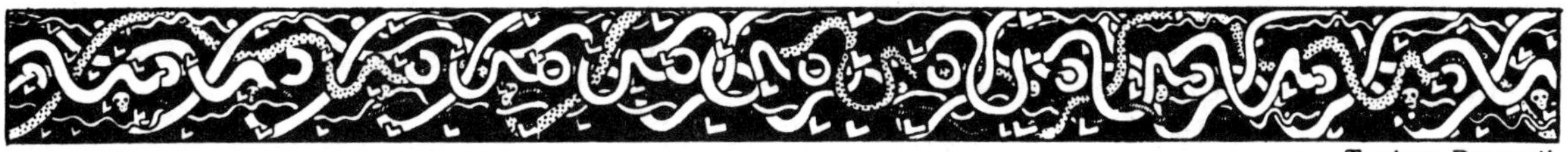

Tucker Petertil

To experiment means "to try", "to test"--ANYTHING! No idea is too outrageous, no medium impossible; no movement incorrect. Experimental zoetroping invites you to discover new and uncoventional ways to set your ideas in motion. As you proceed, keep this in mind: curiosity, creative daring and a willingness to push limits are of primary importance. Let's look at two experimental areas: media and strips.

<u>Experimental Media</u>

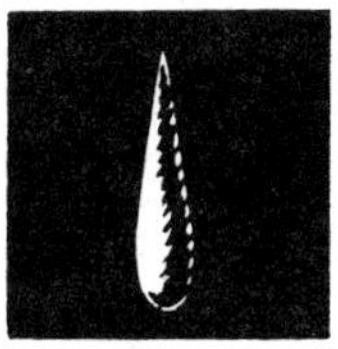

One of the most magical strips I've ever seen showed a plump, white droplet, falling and splashing repeatedly against a jet black background. The strip was powerfully evocative. The droplet seemed to glow. The darkness surrounding it was mysteriously soft. A close examination of the strip revealed that all the droplet and splash shapes had been carefully formed out of white Fimo clay. After the clay was baked, all shapes were carefully glued in place on a piece of black velvet. Said animator Bill Talbot about his unusual strip: "I wanted it to look eerie and three dimensional at the same time". Had the animator merely drawn or painted his shapes on paper the results would have been far less effective. Bill's choice of media made all the difference.

The term "media" suggests any material or substance that can be used to create an image. Experimental media refers to anything above and beyond the conventional felt pens and colored pencils we've already mentioned. The two and three dimensional materials available for zoetroping are mind boggling. Consider the use of the following, and anything else that strikes your fancy:

--2 Dimensional--Magazine cut outs; photographs; Xeroxed pictures (black and white, <u>and</u> color); cloth; tapes (from colored Mystik to silvery <u>duct</u>); Zipatone letters, numbers, dots and symbols; Avery labels; rubber stamp images; glitter; stickers; spray paint; airplane dope; and let's not forget a few of the wilder papers: Origami, tissue, rice and Color Aid...

--3 Dimensional--Yarn; embroidery thread; rope; designer's pins; Q tips; cork; bottle tops; clay; wood; plastic; glass; styrofoam packing pellets; beads; pipe cleaners; buttons; feathers; sea shells; poker chips; Legos; plasticine. (See p. 97.)

With today's super glues ("Yes" paste, Borden's Bond I and II, Barge Cement...) <u>anything</u> can be permanently affixed to a strip. And don't forget: strips need not be made out of paper. (How about felt, fur, acetate, or the highly reflective chrome mylar?)

## Light

Light is another medium that can be used to dramatically transform your strips. Consider these possibilities:

1. Colored light

   Change your white zoetrope strips into gold, lavender or rose with the flick of a switch: use colored light bulbs. They're available in a full range of colors at electrical supply stores and lighting specialty outlets.

2. Black light

   Create strips using fluorescent papers, paints, crayons and chalk. Take your zoetrope into a dark room and illuminate your moving pictures with a black (near ultra-violet) light, and watch your lines and colors take on a weirdly beautiful glow. For a complete list of black light and fluorescent materials see Media p. 95.

3. Light to produce shadows

   Create "relief" zoetrope strips. A "relief" strip is one in which the materials (anything from clay to cork) project away from the strip's surface. Adjust your light source so that when the zoetrope is spinning, you'll see moving shadows as well as motion pictures.

   Affix pieces of transparent colored plastic (or even glass) so that they're perpendicular to the strip's surface and as the strip rotates you'll see colored, kinetic shadows.

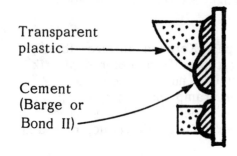

Transparent plastic ⟶

Cement (Barge or Bond II) ⟶

Sideview--"Relief" strip showing protruding shapes

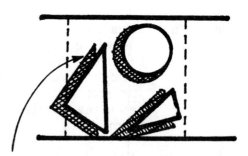

Shadows cast by a "relief" strip

## Experimental Strips

Experimental zoetrope strips, unlike all the strips we've looked at so far, are non-cyclical. This means that frame #12 need not lead logically or gradually back to frame #1. There are three types:

### 1. The "Abrupt" Strip

Progressive changes take place across all 12 frames of the strip. Consequently, frame #1 and #12 will be radically different. Because of the big jump between frames #12 and #1, you'll see an abrupt change each time frame #1 comes into view.

"Abrupt" strips are fine for experiments with progressive change, and for younger children who haven't quite grasped the concept of the cycle.

Lisa Rogers

### 2. The Frameless Strip

Frameless zoetroping, as the name implies, dispenses with the concept of frames altogether. The entire strip becomes fertile ground for images that can be as spontaneous and freewheeling as strip A. below (created by a seven year old) or as controlled and consciously designed as strip B. Since individual frames, progressive change and the cycle are irrelevant when using the frameless approach, predicting motion becomes very difficult. You never know what to expect. Therein lies the great appeal, and the limitation of frameless zoetroping.

Frameless strips are ideal for discovering new images, color experiments and for testing new media. Little kids love them because their drawings--even scribbles--take on a whole new life in the zoetrope.

Allison Macolm

A.

Roger Kukes

B.

### 3. The Crazy Quilt Strip

Distinctly different images are created in each of the 12 frames. Since there is no attempt to present progressive changes, there's no smooth motion. But the viewer will definitely see moving pictures of some sort.

Crazy Quilt strips are great for testing the limits of persistence of vision, and for experimenting with color and texture. Also, they are a fine first step for kid animators learning about frames.

Roger Kukes

### Drum Floor Zoetroping

Somewhere along the line it may have occured to you that animated pictures could be created on the inner drum bottom or "floor" of your zoetrope. This possibility wasn't entirely lost on the makers of zoetropes in the 19th century. While most manufacturers concentrated on the familiar strips we've been discussing, a few provided decorated discs that covered the entire inner drum bottom. When these zoetropes were activated, the viewer saw motion pictures both on the wall and on the floor of the zoetrope.

To quickly see how drum floor zoetroping works, let's create a sample disc:

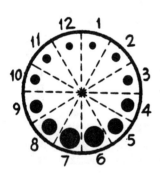

a. draw a circle with a 9 1/2" diameter on a piece of heavy paper or cardboard.

b. using a protractor, divide circle into 12 parts (i.e. 12 frames).

c. work out a cycle of any simple shape--circle, square, rectangle--getting larger and smaller. (You can use the 1-12, 6-7 method.)

d. cut the circle out, place it in the bottom of your zoetrope, light and view.

As you proceed, remember that the experimental spirit invites you to try creating discs every which way--using non-cyclical imagery as well as cyclical, two and three dimensional materials, and light to create shadows and for dramatic effect.

Some of the most effective discs I've seen have been those that relate to or interact with an accompanying zoetrope strip. In one, a series of colorful goemetric shapes marched across a disc and up the side of the zoetrope strip. In another, a series of eleven runners made out of plasticine ran around the disc, while on the zoetrope strip, an animated crowd cheered wildly.

## Tips on Experimental Zoetroping

1. Experimental zoetroping places fewer constraints on your creativity than the other approaches I've discussed. It encourages you to experience the worlds of shape, color, texture, light and motion from the viewpoint of a child--that is, as if you're seeing everything for the first time. Enjoy the freedom, and trust your senses.

2. When experimenting, don't worry about creating the perfect zoetrope strip, or even strips that are "successful". Even if results are not what you expected--you will always learn something.

3. Working with new media often triggers new ideas--ideas that you'd never get using the same old tools and techniques.

4. The true experimenter is primarily interested in the answer to this question: "What will happen if I...?" And there is no way you'll know until you <u>do it</u>! This attitude may not grow hair or make you rich, but it just might help you stay young.

5. "Take chances. That's how great things are born." (James Beard)

66

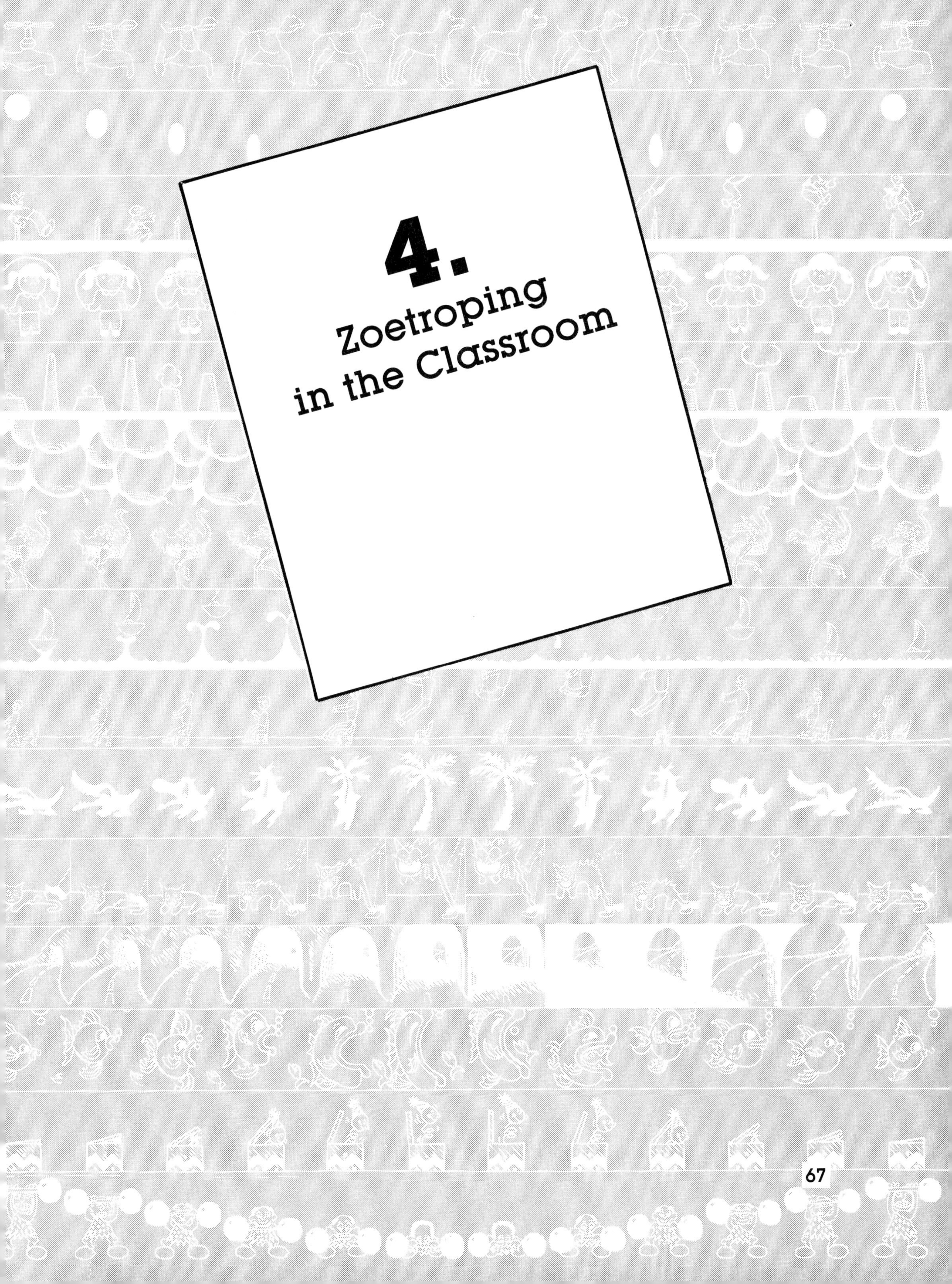

# 4.
# Zoetroping in the Classroom

# A Word to Teachers

When I first started working with the zoetrope in 1978, I thought of it as a great way to teach animation basics--little more. Since that time, I've worked with hundreds of teachers who have enthusiastically suggested ways the zoetrope might be used, not only for fun, but as a unique and powerful teaching tool.

Your work with the zoetrope has probably already suggested many useful projects that you can begin doing with your students. Consulting the learning objectives for your particular level and subject area will suggest many more.

In the following pages you'll find five sample projects. Even if these projects aren't right for your classroom--look them over and you'll glimpse the zoetrope's potential for refreshing and "animating" curriculum. Use these samples as models for projects of your own design.

Before discussing specific projects, let's take a look at some tips that will make it much easier to teach the zoetrope in any classroom.

# Tips on Teaching the Zoetrope

Before attempting to teach the zoetrope, you should be familiar with "The Big Five" and you should try creating a few strips yourself. Simply reading about making strips won't prepare you for even basic questions arising in your classroom. I suggest you try a couple of 1-12, 6-7 strips (see p. 30) and at least one continuous action strip. In addition, the following tips should help.

1. Getting Started

   --When explaining zoetrope basics have everyone gather around a well lit zoetrope (even very large groups). Show different kinds of strips. Seeing is believing and the best motivation possible.

   --Use the short zoetrope (see p. 98) in classrooms where kids are 14 or under. This model will make it relatively easy for even little guys to insert and remove zoetrope strips themselves.

   --Before students create strips relating to curriculum (e.g. strips illustrating "The Evaporation Cycle" or "Animals in Motion"...) they should have the chance to produce a few strips just for fun. These "fun" strips will give them a chance to get a handle on the fundamentals (image making, progressive change, the cycle, etc.).

2. Teaching the Zoetrope at all Levels--What To Expect From Your Students

   --Kindergarten/first graders will probably understand frames only.

   --Second graders may understand frames and progressive change, but not the cycle.

   --Third graders given clear instructions should be able to produce zoetrope strips that demonstrate an understanding of frames, progressive change and the cycle.

   --Fourth graders through adult should be dealing with "The Big Five" (idea, images, progressive change, motion and message) and the cycle.

3. Creating Zoetrope Strips

   All groups 8 years of age and older should follow these steps:

   1. Work out idea on idea paper. That means produce 12 progressively changing pictures that form a cycle.

   2. Draw images in light pencil on a zoetrope strip.

   3. View roughs in the zoetrope.

   4. Make corrections and clean up strip.

   5. Work out color scheme on idea paper.

   6. Add line and color to zoetrope strip.

   7. View and evaluate.

4. Instructor's Role

--Be supportive of all (and especially) first attempts.

--Remind student regularly that "Motion is the key--not drawing 'pretty pictures'". This will alleviate a good deal of anxiety about drawing, and help students focus on the real issue: motion and the cycle.

--You should always look at idea papers before students begin drawing on strips. Before giving your "OK", make sure ideas are clear, changes are gradual enough and that the cycle will work.

--Remind students that outlining their drawings with a black Flair pen will help their images read more clearly. So will the use of light colors against dark and warm against cool.

5. Using the Zoetrope to Stimulate Originality

To stimulate creativity and originality with all groups, start off by showing many different kinds of sample strips (abstract as well as representational). This will alert everyone to the fact that there's room for any and every way of working.

Don't expect first attempts to be great or highly original--just make sure that everyone's working with "The Big Five" and the cycle. Later on, originality should matter and you should say so. With younger children, I routinely discourage obvious solutions and forbid cliches (e.g. Pac Man, and here in the Pacific Northwest, Mt. St. Helen's eruptions). Initially some kids will complain, then surprise themselves (and you) with their terrific ideas.

6. Starting a Zoetrope Strip Collection

A good zoetrope strip is worth a thousand words especially when you're trying to stimulate originality, or explain metamorphosis or lateral motion.

Make copies of the best strips produced by your classes and return the original to the student. Strips can be photocopied (color Xeroxing is available as well as black and white) or simply traced. In no time you will have a great collection of sample strips. They'll withstand the ravages of time and handling if you laminate them.

7. Group Evaluations

End each zoetrope project with an evaluation session. Gather everyone around the zoetrope. Have each student present her/his finished product in turn. Even if strips were created only for fun, there's still a lot to talk about, e.g. "What do you see?..." "Is the motion interesting?".. "Does the cycle work?"...etc.

# Sample Projects

## LIFE STAGES

Subject: Social Studies, Health, Science, Biology

Level: Grades 5-12

Objective:  Learner will demonstrate his/her ability to understand the stages of life--and to represent them as a series of progressively changing pictures.

This project introduces kids to the concept of change in time--specifically to the changes our bodies/faces undergo as we pass through the stages of life. Thanks to the amazin' zoetrope students will be able to view their drawings as animated portraits spanning seventy plus years.

Sue Crawford

Step by Step Instructions for Teaching Life Stages Zoetrope Strips

1. Introduce/discuss the concept of change.

   Encourage students to talk about things that undergo change over a period of time. The bottom line, of course, is this: "Ultimately everything changes, including you and me..."

2. Discuss the stages of life

   Make a list of 12 distinct stages, e.g.--

   | | |
   |---|---|
   | 1. Baby | 7. Adult (mid-late 20's) |
   | 2. Toddler | 8. Mature adult (30's) |
   | 3. Kid (5-6 years) | 9. 40's |
   | 4. Big Kid (11-12 years) | 10. 50's |
   | 5. Adolescent (16-17) | 11. 60's |
   | 6. Young Adult (early 20's) | 12. Old age (70's - 80's) |

3. Look at pictures of faces

   Have students gather pictures of faces from many sources, (magazine images, reproductions of paintings, family photos, etc.) Practice matching faces to specific life stages and talk about the changes that faces undergo as they age.

   --Talk about all parts of the face

   It's important for kids--especially younger ones--to name names: not only "mouth", and "nose", but "eyelid", "nostril", "pupil", etc.

72

4. Practice drawing different kinds of faces

--Have kids look at photos, at themselves in the mirror and at each other. They should try drawing different kinds of faces: all ages, different races and both sexes. Remind them that they are not expected to make perfect drawings, but that--as much as possible--"We should be able to tell it's a toddler, not an old man". Students should draw a minimum of 5 different faces (front view).

Maya Kukes

Since the goal of this project is becoming aware of how faces change over a period of time--not drawing like Michaelangelo or Norman Rockwell--simple drawings are OK. The following sequence will help anyone get a handle on drawing acceptable faces.

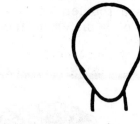

Begin with light pencil and draw the basic shape of the head.

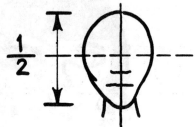

Locate lines for eyes, nose, mouth, ears, hair...(eyes are slightly higher than 1/2 way between the top of the head and the bottom of the chin).

Lightly sketch in features. Use simple shapes.

Make shapes more definite so that a particular face begins to come into focus.

Finalize features and add details that make the face look distinctive-ly "toddler", "adolescent" or 60 year old.

When features and details are estab-lished, erase extraneous lines and go over with a black Flair pen.

5. Select a face to represent the 12 stages of life

Any face is OK, though the most interesting subject might be the student him/herself. If doing a self-portrait, student should look at baby pictures to see what she used to look like, and at older siblings, parents, grandparents to see what s/he might look like in the future.

6. Draw faces on the zoetrope strip.

    a. Draw only the face shapes--one in each frame

        --Shapes should begin to reflect a particular life stage. (Rounder shapes usually suggest younger chidren, especially babies; narrower-longer faces usually suggest older folks.)

        --Shapes should fill the frame. (Tiny heads won't work.) At this stage, strips should look something like the example below.

    b. Work out all 12 faces

        --Each face should represent a distinct life stage--like the ones discussed on p. 72 (e.g. frame #1 - baby; frame #2 - toddler; frame #3 - Kid, 5-6 years...).

        --The key to success is to make each drawing slightly different, yet make all drawings look like the same person.

        --Check the 12 faces in a well lit zoetrope. Since the face in frame #12 will be very different than the one in frame #1, don't expect to see a cycle. Still, you should see one face going through its changes, not a bunch of totally unrelated faces.

        --Once students are satisfied with the drawings, they should go over the pencil lines with a black Flair pen, and color the background (coloring the background will help faces show up better).

7. Evaluate

    Use the following as criteria for evaluating "Life Stages" strips: Hold up the strip outside the zoetrope and ask:

        --Does each face in each frame represent a different stage of life? Which drawings work best and why?

    View the strip in a <u>slowly</u> spinning zoetrope and ask:

        --Do we see the same person's face getting progressively older?

Roger Kukes

75

# SIGHT WORD ZOETROPE STRIPS

Subject: Language Arts (Reading)

Level: Created by Grades 5-8; Used by K--3

Objective: Learner will demonstrate his ability to create a cyclical zoetrope strip containing both moving pictures and legible words. The word and picture message should be identical. Completed strips will be used by primary students to improve their word recognition.

This project is an exercise in using the zoetrope to integrate words and moving pictures. It also offers upper elementary students the opportunity to directly assist younger children.

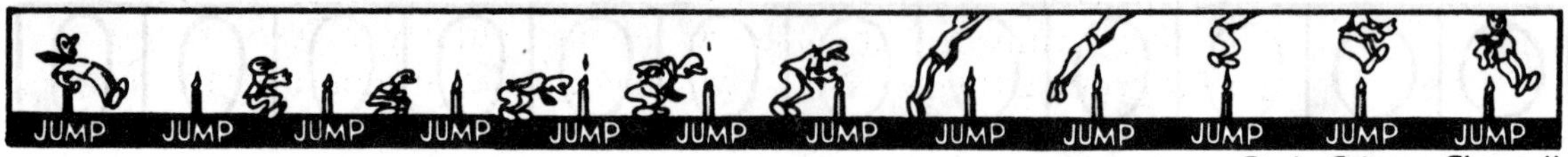
JUMP JUMP JUMP JUMP JUMP JUMP JUMP JUMP JUMP JUMP JUMP JUMP

Cindy Stinson-Chennell

Step by Step Instructions for Teaching Sight Word Strips

1. Explain the project
    a. Show examples--if possible. (Nothing explains it better.)
    b. Make sure everyone understands the reason for making the strips. ("They'll actually be used by little kids to help them improve their reading...")
    c. Students should choose nouns (e.g. pencil, dog, house...) or action words (e.g. run, sleep, eat...) to animate. (A primary level teacher might even drop in and suggest appropriate words.)
    d. Remind students that their images will always be more engaging if they move in some way, e.g. pencils might rotate, dogs bark or wag tails, houses have smoke coming out of their chimneys.
    e. As students begin to develop their ideas, they'll need to make both words and pictures easy to see. The following should help.

        --The ratio of picture to word should be about 2:1

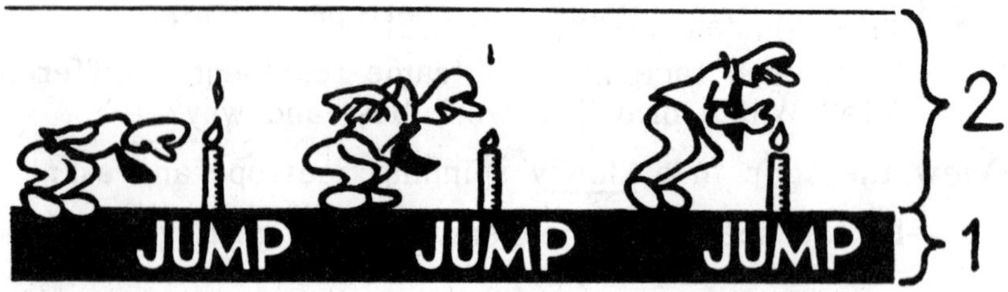
JUMP JUMP JUMP
2
1

        --Fatter letters will read more clearly than skinny ones.

        --Words should be printed in the same location in each frame. To facilitate this, students can letter their word

in a square the size of a zoetrope frame--then carefully
trace the word in all 12 frames.

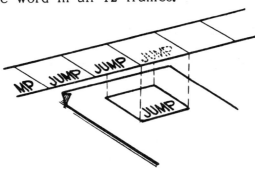

f. Representing human motion can be tricky, but if students "walk
through" the proposed action and breakdown movements logically, surprisingly good results can be achieved--even by those
who don't think of themselves as particularly gifted in the
drawing department. Also, whenever your students draw people,
they should be encouraged to use figures made up of interlocking shapes--not just stick figures.

2. Students produce strips

a. They should follow the steps under "Tips on Teaching the Zoetrope"--#3.

b. The older kids might produce their finished strips in black
line. That way they'll be easy to photocopy. When the strips
reach the primary youngsters, they can add color. As they
color the strips, the word-picture relationship will be nat-
urally (and repeatedly) reinforced.

3. Evaluate completed sight word strips

Use these as criteria for measuring a strip's success:

--Does the motion cycle work?

--Are both words and pictures easy to see?

--Do words and pictures convey the same message?

--Are the moving pictures fun to watch?

4. Deliver completed sight word strips to the primary classroom(s).

Have the creators of the strips actually visit the classroom(s) of
the younger children, both to present the strips and to demonstrate
the mechanics of the zoetrope.

# COLOR WHEEL ZOETROPING

Subject: Visual Art

Level: Grade 4--Adult

Objective: Learner will demonstrate his ability to produce a zoetrope strip that sets the colors of the color wheel in motion.

Designers and artists know that color can delight or disturb the eye; architects know that color can make the spaces we live and work in seem larger and smaller, warmer and cooler; and psychologists, that color profoundly affects our moods. With art specialists rapidly disappearing from many elementary schools, kids are learning almost nothing about color. Sadly, informed, expressive or divergent uses of color are seldom valued or validated in the classroom. Usually by grade three or four youngsters have become stilted and predictable in their color choices: skies are automatically blue, horses--brown, clouds--white.

This project has a dual purpose. First, it teaches the rudiments of color. Second, it offers students the chance to utilize color as a dynamic phenomenon--a phenomenon promising splendor and surprise.

Step by Step Instructions for Teaching Color Wheel Zoetroping

1. Explain the color wheel

    --Draw a diagram similar to the one below. Identify the 3 primary colors (red, yellow, blue), the 3 secondary colors (violet, green, orange) and the mixtures of these two color groups (Yellow-Orange ...Red-Orange...Red-Violet, etc.).

    --Identify warm (yellows, oranges, reds) and cool colors (violets, blues, greens).

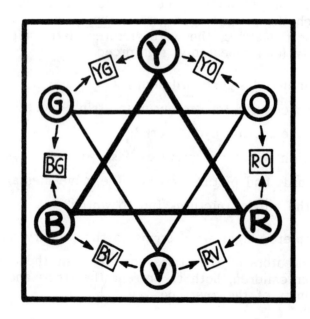

2. Each student creates her/his own color wheel

It should duplicate the diagram you drew and be produced in full color. Any media will do. Felt tip markers are the easiest to handle. Colors are clean and bright--No muss, no fuss. (My students have had great success working with Marvy Markers-- see p. 95.)

Though paint (water colors, tempra, acrylics) has obvious disadvantages (it can be messy and the project will take longer), there's no better medium for mixing colors. If your students have the experience of mixing all their colors using only the three primaries, they'll really understand the whys and wherefores of the color wheel.

Each color should be labeled and given a number. It's best if everyone uses the same numbering system--Yellow--#1; Yellow-Orange--#2; Orange--#3...

1
yellow
2
yel-or
3
orange
4
red orange
5
red
6
red violet
7
violet
8
blue violet
9
blue
10
blue green
11
green
12
yellow green

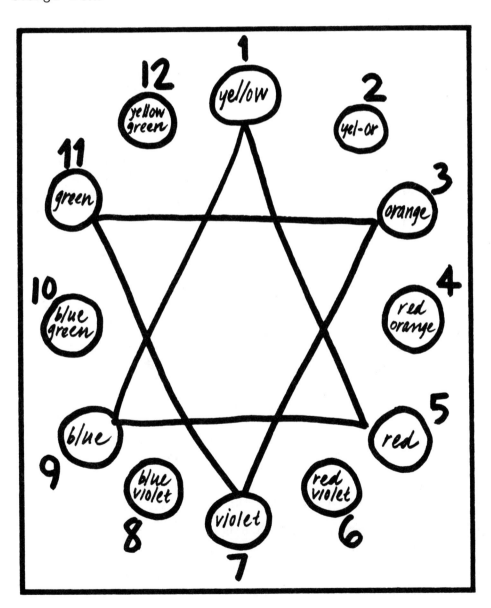

## 3. Explain Color Cycles

Have students notice how colors change gradually as their eyes move around the color wheel--and that the last color, green-yellow (#12) leads logically back to the first, yellow (#1)--thus creating a cycle.

Tell them that the strips they will be producing should be fully colored, and that each and every shape in all frames should be part of some kind of color cycle. Backgrounds too can be colored cyclically--or they can be one color. (Either way will work.) The numbers in the diagrams below represent the colors of the color wheel described on p. 78.

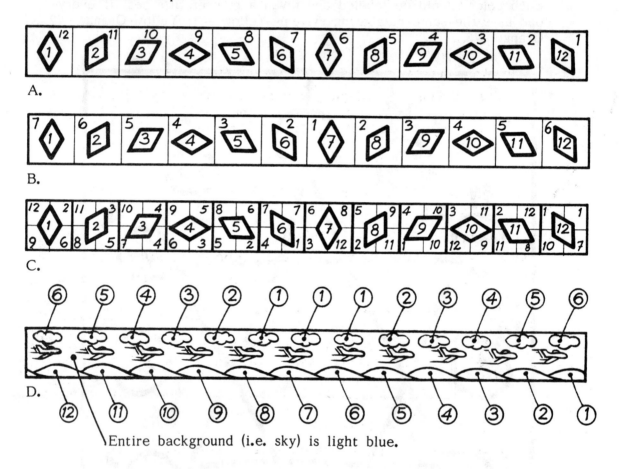

A.

B.

C.

D.

Entire background (i.e. sky) is light blue.

Looking at strips A-D above, follow the progress of each shape as it changes from frame to frame. Notice that all the shapes are part of some sort of color cycle (with the exception of the background in D). Notice too, that cycles don't have to use all 12 colors of the color wheel (e.g. the background in example B.).

In strip D., the airplane shape (though unnumbered here) goes through a color cycle in the original strip.

If possible, make copies of some or all of the above strips. This is one of those occasions where a few sample strips may be worth a thousand words.

4. Students design strips

Before going to work, remind students that any subject is acceptable (cars, animals, faces, abstract shapes...) as long as both their moving pictures and their changing colors are worked out to form cycles.

A. Idea paper

As you begin to "ideate", remember that color will be just as important as kinetics. Play with a few ideas before selecting one.

B. Draw images in light pencil on zoetrope strips

C. View pencil "roughs" in the zoetrope

D. Make corrections and "clean up"

E. Work out color coded cycles on the strip.

Write numbers in light pencil in each shape that's to be colored as in the examples A-D on the previous page. Students decide at this stage if background is to be one color or part of a color cycle.

F. Color zoetrope strip

Students "color by number". Insist on meticulous craftsmanship:

--work slowly and carefully

--fully color each shape before proceeding to the next

--cover up all the white of the paper

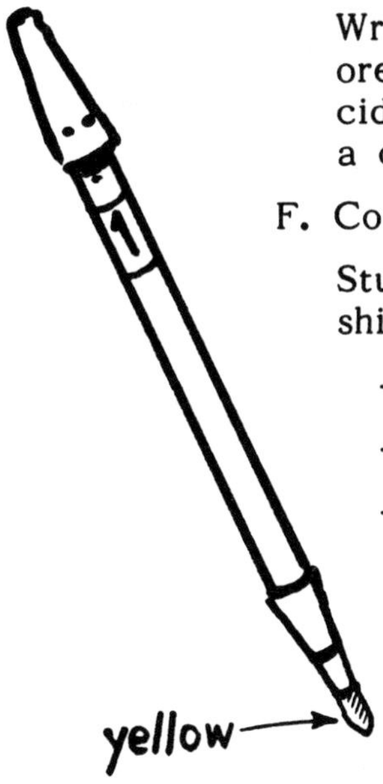
1
yellow

> A sure way of avoiding color accidents ("Oh no! I colored this shape the wrong color!") is to put numbers right on the barrel of the felt pen--or on the side of the paint jar.

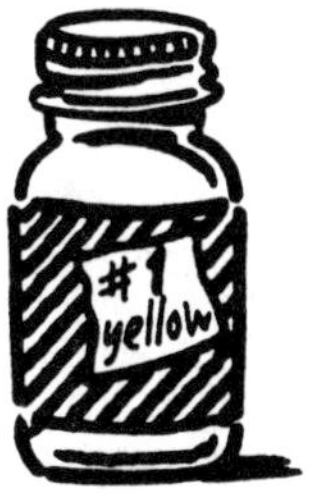
#1
yellow

4. View and evaluate completed strips

Use these as criteria for measuring a strip's success:

--Does the motion cycle work?

--Do the color cycles work? (Are they complete?)

--Is this the most successful version of the strip? Is there any way it might be improved?

# VISUAL/VERBAL COMMUNICATION

Level: Grade 5-College

Objective: Student will demonstrate his/her ability to communicate a definite message to others using both words and moving pictures.

Clear, intentional, unambiguous communication is a primary goal in most areas of the curriculum. More than that, it's the keystone of all human relationships. Inexplicably, it's a subject that's seldom addressed directly. This project not only introduces basic communication concepts, it gives students the opportunity to test their communication skills.

Here's how it works. Each student communicator creates a written statement and a full color zoetrope strip. The statement and the strip should convey exactly the same message. Messages are to be kept secret.

Upon completion, the class will view each strip and try and "get the message". The communicator will then read her statement; the messages conveyed by the statement and the strip will be compared and evaluated.

Step by Step Instructions for Teaching Visual/Verbal Communication Strips

1. Explain the primary objectives of the project and these basic communication concepts:

   communicator--someone who has a message to convey to others.

   message--the idea(s) being conveyed.

   receiver--one at whom the message is aimed.

2. Student selects a subject

   Student begins to zero in on a specific idea. The idea can be any concept, action, experience or emotion. The student shouldn't tell anyone (except the teacher) the idea.

3. Student creates the written statement

   It should be a concise verbal description of what the student is trying to convey, and what the receiver ought to get when he/she views the zoetrope strip.

   Here's a sample statement and its accompanying strip.

   "Diving has always been my favorite sport. I took lessons when I was about seven. In my strip I want to show myself going off the board, making a big arc--then disappearing into the water with a huge splash." (5th grader)

Maya Kukes

82

In the ingenious strip below illustrating "wasting time watching TV", 7th grader Marc Pearlman has employed four moving elements to help deliver his message. The kid lies on a bed eating incessantly while the TV blares. The passage of time is represented both by the rapid rotation of the clock's hands, and the large window changing from day to night.

And here's part of Marc's statement.

"Sometimes I watch way too much TV and my brain feels like jello. What I want to convey is how it feels to waste your time watching the tube..."

4. Research

Student is responsible for doing whatever is necessary to create the most vivid, accurate and/or expressive zoetrope strip. This might include reading, looking at pictures, or sketching objects or actions to be used in the strip.

5. Students produce strips

Strips should be created in the usual manner (See Tips on Teaching the Zoetrope--#3.)

6. Communicate

   a. the <u>communicator</u> shows his/her finished strip to the class. No talking--no verbal communication of any kind is allowed. The strip should speak for itself.

   b. the <u>receivers</u> view the strip and after careful consideration offer "feedback" to the <u>communicator,</u> i.e. tell him what the strip says to them.

   During this time of communication, it's important to encourage open, honest discussion, differing viewpoints, and accurate perceptions based on the information being conveyed <u>only</u> by the strip.

   c. the <u>communicator</u> reads his/her statement to the group.

7. Evaluate

During evaluation, these questions should be discussed:

--Does the strip deliver a clear <u>message</u>?

--Do the written statement and the zoetrope strip say the same thing?

--If not, how could the zoetrope strip be changed to more accurately reflect the content of the statement?

# ANIMALS IN MOTION

Subject: Science, Art, History

Level: Grade 3--Adult

Objective: Learner will demonstrate her/his ability to create a cyclical zoetrope strip using a moving animal as subject.

The zoetrope is an ideal place to introduce any topic relating to animals and the animal kingdom. In fact, the "zoe" in zoetrope literally means animal (from the Greek--"zoin"). Few people really see or understand the way animals move. By breaking movements down into a series of incremental steps, students of all ages will begin to appreciate the beauty and diversity of animal locomotion.

Some types of animal motion are easier to represent than others. A third grader would have little trouble portraying a bird opening and closing its beak, but it might take a conscientious eighth grader to successfully animate a hopping frog, and a high school sophomore to tackle a cantering horse. To facilitate teaching animal motion at all levels, simple, intermediate and advanced projects are described below.

Simple Animal Motion Strips (Grades 3--6)

Simple animal zoetroping asks students to practice drawing different kinds of animals--then create a strip where a specific animal does something-- anything <u>except</u> run, walk, gallop, etc. (These are discussed in the intermediate and advanced sections.) Subjects for simple strips might include an elephant raising and lowering its trunk; a turtle moving its head in and out of its shell; or a peacock spreading its tail feathers. Brainstorming with your group will yield many more possibilities. Eventually, you might also want to include imaginary animals, dinosaurs and mythical creatures like dragons, sea monsters, griffins and unicorns.

Diane LaRoche

Step by Step Instructions for Teachings Simple Animal Motion

1. View and discuss pictures of animals

   Show pictures, slides and movies of every kind. Have students notice and describe the characteristics that make a particular animal unique e.g. the giraffe's long neck, brown spots, small antlers and skinny legs. Make sure their descriptions are specific. Better yet, have them write down three or four characteristics for each animal.

2. Practice drawing different kinds of animals

This important practice phase is designed to support every child's effort to draw a reasonable likeness of a particular animal.

   A. Have students look at photographs, paintings and drawings of real animals and copy these. (Drawings shouldn't be done from memory or imagination.) Remind students that they're not expected to make perfect drawings, but that--as much as possible --"We should be able to tell that it's a bear and not a beaver".

   B. Have students fill up large pieces of paper with drawings of the entire animal--not just the head.

S. Crawford/M. Kukes

C. Though many children have their own inimitable way of drawing (and should be left alone), some will seek your guidance. Following this simple sequence will help <u>anyone</u> improve his/her drawings:

Begin with light pencil lines to establish the basic length and height of the animal. (Stick figures are OK.)

Flesh out lines so that they form interlocking shapes. (Pencil)

Refine lines and shapes so that a particular animal begins to come into focus.

Finalize. Add dark outline (I suggest using a black Flair pen) and color (colored pencils, or fine tipped felt pens...please no crayons).

Color is crucial in terms of aiding recognizability. (It's the difference between a tabby cat and a tiger--or a horse and a zebra.)

D. Enthusiastically support and validate each student's efforts. Be very vocal. Hold up examples of work in progress--especially the drawings of kids who don't have a lot of natural ability but who are really trying. Congratulate them on their fine work publicly.

3. Select an animal to set in motion

Having completed drawings of animals at rest, it's time for students to think about selecting an animal for their zoetrope strips. Ideally, each child should choose a different animal. Students should select an animal they can draw fairly well, and brainstorm different ways the animal might move.

4. Idea paper

Using the 1-12, 6-7 method, students should work out all twelve increments of their idea. Check the increments to make sure they form a cycle.

5. Draw images on a blank zoetrope strip in light pencil.

6. View strip in the zoetrope and make necessary corrections.

7. Clean up the strip.

8. Work out a color scheme on the idea paper.

9. Finalize the strip.

Add outline and color.

10. View and evaluate.

Use these as criteria for measuring a strip's success:

A. Do we know what kind of animal it is?

B. Can we see clearly what the animal is doing?

C. Does the cycle work?

## Intermediate Animal Motion Strips (Grades 6--Adult)

Intermediate Animal Zetroping invites students to create strips in which two or four legged animals walk, hop, canter, gallop and run. Creating cyclical motion of animal legs can be tricky--but with the help of a remarkable book, anyone with average drawing ability and the willingness to do simple problem solving should produce admirably.

The book I'm referring to is "Animals in Motion" by Edweard Muybridge (see BOOKS--p. 112). This monumental photographic work, produced at the University of Pennsylvania between 1884-85, contains detailed motion sequences of scores of animals including galloping horses, jumping kangaroos, trotting deer and strutting ostriches. It is the indispensable guide for anyone wishing to do or teach animal motion. Without it--you'll only be guessing.

When tackling intermediate animal motion, choose those sequences in "Animals in Motion" that show one stride (i.e. a cycle) in 10-13 pictures. Any of these will work in our zoetrope. A 12 image cycle will show an animal moving in place, while a 10, 11 or 13 will move laterally.

Step by Step Instructions for Teaching Intermediate Animal Motion

Locate usable cycles

1. Find as many one stride photographic sequences of 10-13 phases in "Animals in Motion" as possible. Xerox these, and make them available to students for reference purposes. As an example, look at Plate 67 --Galloping Horse in 12 phases. It'll work beautifully.

2. Test the cycle

   In order to test a particular cycle, have students trace the photographs from their Xerox in order on to a blank zoetrope strip. (If the motion sequence has 10, 11 or 13 increments, have them use the Lateral Motion Guide to insure accurate placement.) Since the goal is to make sure the cycle is working, images must be traced accurately. (Simple sillouettes are OK.)

   Test in the zoetrope. If the cycle works, go on to #3. If it doesn't, student will have to figure what went wrong and fix it.

3. Students design their own animal

   The goal here is to come up with a unique version of a particular animal--and not merely a quick copy or tracing of Muybridges' photographs. Have students look at different types of animal pictures-- slides, photos, films. If possible they should also view images of animals by artists of various cultures and from different historical periods. Though some students of limited drawing ability will do well to create strips where the viewer can recognize his animal as "a cat" many students will relish the opportunity to examine and draw from a full range of visual styles--not only realism, but abstraction, caricature and cartoons. Animal idiosyncracy should always be encouraged. Say to everyone: "Make your horse or elephant or ostrich as special as you can".

Sue Crawford

4. Student draws rough increments of his/her animal on a blank zoetrope strip.

   Once a satisfactory design for an animal has been worked out, the student should draw the increments of his/her animal rough on a strip using the images from the Xerox as a guide for the location of the legs.

5. Finalize strip

   Check roughs in the zoetrope and if the cycle looks good, finalize strips in the usual manner (i.e. dark outline and full color).

Above: Strip based on Plate 67--Galloping Horse by M. Kukes - age 12.

6. Evaluate

   Use the criteria for evaluating simple animal strips. (See p. 88, #10) When appropriate, add this question: Is the animal special and unique?


## Advanced Animal Motion Strips

Advanced animal zoetroping challenges you and your students to use Muybridge's "Animal Motion" as a basic guide for the design of <u>any</u> animal motion cycle.

Great as "Animal Motion" is, it's flawed from the zoetroper's point of view because many of the book's motion sequences are presented in more or fewer increments than the 10-13 that will work best in our zoetrope.

In order to adapt just about <u>any</u>* of the Muybridge sequences, students should--

1. Choose an animal and a sequence that really interests them and study it carefully. Special attention should be paid to the progressive changes that each body part goes through--especially the legs-- as the animal moves through its cycle (one stride).

2. Begin laying down roughs on a blank zoetrope strip. (Stick figures are OK at this stage.) Keep referring to the photographic sequence and note that:

   --in sequences where <u>more</u> increments are provided than the required 12 (e.g. Plate 165--Galloping American Bison--one stride

---

*Some animal motion cycles (for instance a very slow walk) may need many more increments than the 12 available to us to be really convincing.

90

in 16 phases), changes will have to be made that are larger than those pictured.

--in sequences where fewer increments are provided than the required 12 (e.g. Plate 166--Kangaroo Jumping--one stride in nine phases), changes will have to be made that are smaller than those pictured.

A good way for students to make sure their cycle is on track would be to see if the animal is approximately half way through its stride at zoetrope frame #6.

3. Check roughs in the zoetrope often and make the necessary corrections. Students shouldn't expect to get everything moving smoothly and cyclically the first time--and like all good animators, they'll do a lot of erasing.

4. Once students are satisfied with their kinetics, they can design their own animal. (See p. 89, #3).

5. Finalize strips.

Here's a finished strip based on Plate 182--"Ostrich Walking." Animator Betty Bethune converted the 10 phase stride presented by Muybridge into a 12 increment continuous action cycle. (Notice how frame #12 leads logically into frame #1.)

Betty Bethune

# 5.
## Mixed Bag

# Media

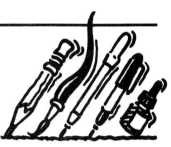

As I've already said, you don't need fancy materials to create successful strips. One of my oldest friends prides himself on being able to consistently produce great images from the crummiest materials he can find (his kids' broken crayons, pencils that are 1/2" long, Bic pens he finds on buses, etc.). If you're short on funds or don't have/or can't get the brands I'm about to mention, don't worry. Just use whatever's on hand.

Still, people in classes and workshops do ask me about media. It's nice to know what's available, so here goes. Most of the materials listed below can be purchased at art supply stores (A), office supply outlets (O), and sometimes at variety stores (V) like K-Mart or Newberry's. Most of the items are pretty cheap. The list doesn't attempt to be exhaustive and obviously reflects my preferences.

## Felt Tip Pens and Markers

Flair Pens    The ones <u>with</u> the plastic point guard. The line thickness is swell; not too thick or thin. (A-O-V)

Marvy Markers    60 colors. Two nib sizes. (Medium and fine). Medium works well for most strips. Pentel also makes a comparable line of markers--fine points only. (A)

Design Markers    Manufactured by Eberhard Faber. Three points: a) Chisled (fairly wide and flat, comes in 96 colors; b) pointed (48 colors) and c)ultra fine--48 colors. Juicy, free-flowing, lovely lacquer based colors. Water resistant. The fumes will make hair grow on your tongue. Open a window when you use them. (A)

Sharpies    Six colors. Permanent. Water resistant. Highly recommended for heavy weight lines. (A-O-V)

## Water Color

Luma    Brilliant, liquid colors available in 1 oz. eye dropper bottles. Can be "erased" by applying laundry bleach with a Q-Tip. Most colors will fade in time and bright light. Dr. Martins makes a comparable line. (A)

Ink

Higgins India or Higgins Black Magic come in 1 oz. eye dropper bottles. Black Magic is the blackest. (A-O-V)

Designer's White  A water soluble, opaque white that will help you touch up mistakes. Better than Liquid Paper and cheaper. Made by Windsor Newton, and Grumbacher in tubes. Luma's "Bleed Proof White" will cover anything. (A)

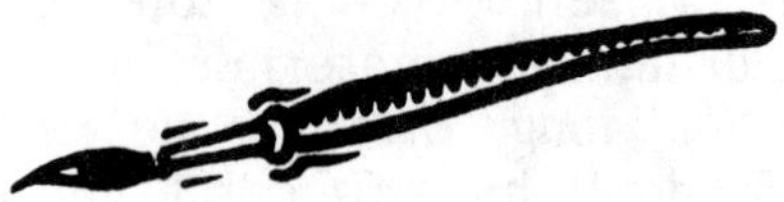

Paint Brushes  If you like to paint, I recommend using red sable water color brushes. Properly cared for (wash after each use in luke warm water and mild soap) they will last a long time. Made by Grumbacher or Windsor Newton. Bigger brushes are great for laying down large areas of color quickly. They can be very EXPENSIVE. However, if you're serious, they're worth the investment. (A)

Colored Pencils

Verithin by Berol  48 colors. Hard lead. Lovely to look at and to use. Great for mixing and shading. Covers bumpy papers well. (A-O)

Prismacolor by Berol  60 colors. Soft leads. Creamy, intense, highly saturated color. Mixes well with Verithin and other Prismacolor pencils. Spectracolor pencils by Venus are very similar. (A-O)

Fluorescent Media

Black Light  A 75 watt bulb made by Yorkville can be found at many lighting specialty stores for around $3. Steer clear of fluorescent tubes. They will certainly work, but can cost $20 or more. In a pinch look for a 250 watt incandescent bulb by General Electric. (Follow manufacturer's instructions to avoid overheating.)

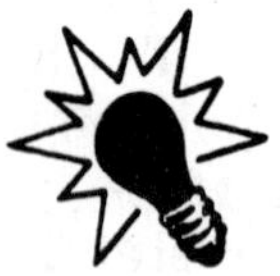

Paints  Both Prang (American Crayon Company) and Crayola produce an inexpensive, six color set of tempra paints. (A-V)

Cartoon Colour Company produces 10 "radiant", fluorescent, polymer acrylic base colors. Available in 2 oz. plastic bottles. Expensive. Send for their color card: 9024 Lindblade St., Culver City, CA 90230.

Crayons  A box of eight is available from Prang and Crayola. (A-V)

Markers  Many manufacturers make them. Look for Sanford's line called "Major Accent". They come in eight waterbase colors and two tip widths: broad and narrow. (O)

Pastels  A box of 12 colors is available from Alphacolor. (A)

## Glues

**Barge Cement** Will bond anything to anything <u>forever</u> (as long as the surfaces are dry and clean). When making your zoetrope, this is the glue you want to use to affix your ice cream drum to the turntable. Some hardware stores carry it. I buy mine at the local Birkenstock shoe store.

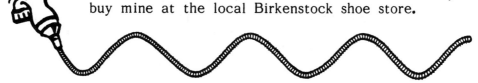

**Yes Paste** Book binding glue. As far as I'm concerned, this is <u>the</u> glue for paper. Anything else will wrinkle or yellow papers. (A) If you have trouble finding it, ask your favorite art supply outlet to order some: "Yes" c/o Gane Brothers & Lane, Inc., 218 Littlefield Avenue, So. San Francisco, CA 94080.

**Elmer's Craft Bond II** A good choice for adhering plastics, foils and fabrics to porous and semi-porous surfaces. (V)

<u>Paper</u> (for strips) See Section II "Preparing Zoetrope Strips", p. 18.

## Clay

**Fimo** Manufactured by Eberhard Faber. This modeling material can be formed into three dimensional shapes, baked in your kitchen oven and glued to zoetrope strips. It's permanent once baked and is available in a full range of colors. Find it at hobby and toy stores.

**Crayola Modeling Clay or Plasticine (by Colorforms)**

Both brands are "oil" base clays. They will not harden. They are very malleable and can be used to make quick three dimensional models to help you visualize tricky changes. Especially good for spatial animation and metamorphosis. Available at variety and toy stores.

# Zoetropes Galore

## ZOETROPES, ZOETROPES . . .

Nineteenth century zoetropes were usually made out of metal. Some were hand cranked. Most rotated smoothly on a spindle base. Todays zoetropes are being made out of wood, plastics (plexiglass and PVC sewer pipe) and good old cardboard. The smallest zoetrope I've ever seen had a circumference of only six inches. The slits were cut into the strip itself; it was attached to a plastic spray can top with a thumb tack. The largest zoetrope I've seen had eighty frames and was mounted on a bicycle wheel. The wheel was placed horizontally on a table and spun on its central axis. I'm certain larger zoetropes exist. If not, they could. How about one the size of a carousel or better still--a water tower.

## THE SHORT ZOETROPE

There's another zoetrope you should know about. It's very similar to the standard zoetrope described on p. 15 except that It's 3 inches shorter. This is the model I normally use. I find that it's easier to insert and remove strips. (So will children 14 and younger.)

--Supplies

Use exactly the same supplies and materials listed on p. 15.

--Step by Step Instructions

1. Measure and Cut

   Measure and cut your drum according to the diagram below.

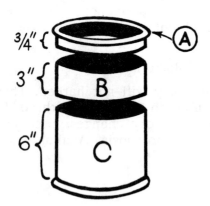

Retain sections A and C

Discard section B

2. Cut Section A.

   Make a series of cuts perpendicular to the metal ring at approximately 2" intervals all around the drum. (On many drums the lines are already impressed on the surface.)

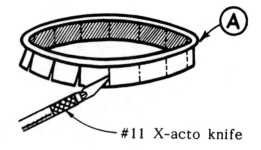

#11 X-acto knife

### 3. Glue Sections A and C

Use Elmer's glue to join sections A and C together. Alternately glue tabs to the inside (I) and the outside (O) of the drum. (It's easiest if you put glue on all tabs at once: spread glue on the <u>back</u> of all the "O" tabs.)

Once you've got glue on all the tabs, set section A down on top of section C as shown in the diagram below.

Press the tabs to the side of the drum with your fingers until the glue sets. When the glue dries (3-5 hours), your short zoetrope will have the strength and stability of the standard zoetrope.

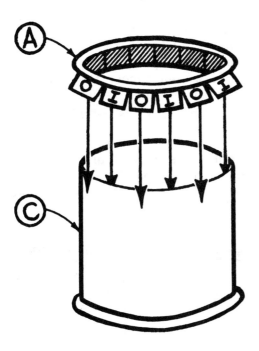

### 4. Complete the Zoetrope

Follow directions on p. 15-17 to complete your zoetrope. You can glue it to the standard 10 1/2" Rubbermaid turntable or the 10 1/2" twin shelf turntable (also made by Rubbermaid). The double shelf model may be easier for little guys (under 8) to spin.

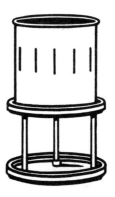

Above: The Short Zoetrope mounted on a twin shelf turntable. Grip the columns and spin.

# ECCENTRIC SLITS

Shortly after he began experimenting with the zoetrope in the late 1970's, University of Oregon art professor Ken O'Connell noticed that the pictures he drew were slightly distorted in a spinning zoetrope. (Circles tended to become ovals, squares compressed into rectangles, and vertical lines were noticably thinner than horizontals.) The vertical shape of the slit seemed to be exerting some influence on the image. (To see this curious phenomenen yourself, draw 12 identical squares or circles across a strip and view in a zoetrope under a bright light.)

Since the normal (vertical) slit caused a slight distortion of the image, O'Connell wondered what would happen if the shapes of the slits were altered intentionally. This led Ken and his students to build a series of zoetropes having eccentrically shaped slits. In one, the 12 slits were cut at a 45° angle. All the pictures viewed in it leaned noticeably: telephone poles, houses and fences were slanted or tipped, and rain that normally fell straight down, now fell diagonally. In another experiment, animator Pierre Dunn created a simple drawing of a Hawaiian dancer that was exactly the same in all 12 frames. Of course it didn't move in a regular zoetrope, but in Dunn's specially designed "wiggle slit" zoetrope, the viewer saw an energetic Hula dancer.

Clearly, the possiblities for creating different kinds of slits are unlimited. Though it may be pretty hard to predict how a particular shape will alter or distort your images--you can be sure of one thing: you'll be able to look at all your old strips and see them in new ways.

Though your slits may be "eccentrically" shaped, try and cut them so they are not too wide. (Try and keep them under 1/8".) Remember--the wider the slit, the more blurry the image--especially under bright light.

# Motorized Zoetropes

Most people are perfectly content to spin their zoetropes manually. With a little practice you can keep a zoetrope spinning smoothly for long periods without fatigue, and varying speeds is a snap. Still, there's no denying it; this is the age of the calculator, Cuisinart and golf cart. We like machines to lighten our load. Why not a motorized zoetrope? Here are a couple of ways to easily set your zoetrope in motion mechanically.

## RECORD PLAYER ZOETROPING

The simplest way to motorize a zoetrope is with a record player or stereo turntable. Make a small hole in the center of the bottom of the zoetrope drum. Then place the drum so that the record spindle fits snugly through the hole. The advantages to this type of zoetroping are pretty obvious. The disadvantages are these:

Record Spindle

--No variable speed. You have to learn to live with the standard 45 or 78 revolutions per minute. (33 1/3 is usually a bit slow.)

--Turntables rotate in a clockwise direction. If you design your strips the usual way (beginning at left and working to the right), you'll find that your strips are going backwards. With some strips this won't matter too much. With others it most certainly will.

There are a couple of things you can do to overrule the problems raised by the clockwise rotation of the turntable:

A. Design your strips from right to left. Just think of the far right frame as #1, and the extreme left frame as #12 as in the diagram below.

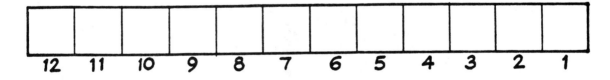

B. Literally change the direction of the turntable

Depending on the machine, going this route can be a hassle or a breeze. I suggest picking up a cheap belt driven model at a second hand store. (Kiddie victrolas are an excellent choice.) Before working on it, always unplug the machine. With a screwdriver and pliers you should be able to get to the turntable mechanism and find the belt drive. Once found, twist the belt to form a figure eight. This will change the direction of the turntable from clockwise to counterclockwise motion. (See diagram below.)

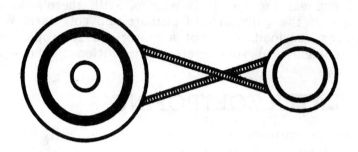

There's another option available if you want to motorize your zoetrope: Put together your own motor. You say you don't know the difference between a battery and a bat? Don't be scared off. The following motor can be assembled by any patient nine year old.

## THE SIMPLE ZOETROPE MOTOR

For the handy-person virtually any small motor (windshield wiper, record player, shaded pole...) can be rigged to rotate the Rubbermaid turntable. Since most of us aren't particularly handy or simply don't have the time or inclination to run around to junkyards and hardware stores, let me introduce you to a motor that's a snap to assemble. It was designed by visual artist Jim Samuels. Samuels challenged himself to find all the parts at one location (Radio Shack), use only household tools for assembly, and keep the entire cost under seven bucks. And now, ladies and gentlemen, Samuels' small miracle!

1. The Motor

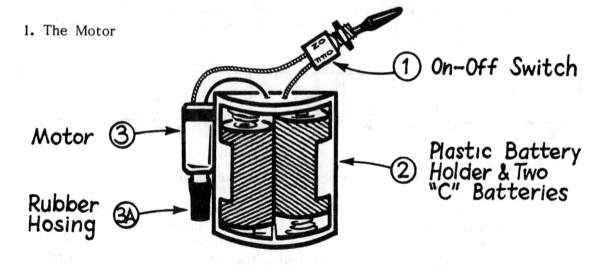

① On-Off Switch
Motor ③
Plastic Battery Holder & Two "C" Batteries ②
Rubber Hosing 3A
ON
OFF

## 2. How it works

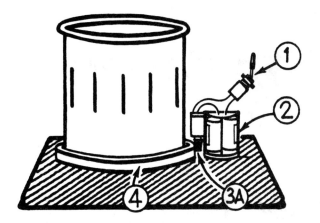

Place the zoetrope on a nonskid surface. (A rubber place mat should do nicely.) Switch motor (1) on. Push rotating rubber tube (3A) against the side of the Rubbermaid turntable (4). As the rubber drive wheel rotates, it causes the turntable to spin.

## 3. Parts

All parts--with the exception of 3A--are from Radio Shack; catalogue numbers are in parenthesis.

(1) On/off toggle switch (#275-324)

(2) Plastic Battery Holder (#270-385) and two "C" batteries

(3) Motor (Direct Current) (#273-222)

(3A) Rubber Hosing

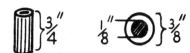

(Pick up at any auto supply store.)

## 4. Assembly

1. Push 3/4" hosing (3A) over drive-wheel of the motor (3) so that the hosing is secure.

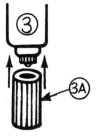

2. Glue motor (3) to battery pack (2) as in diagram below.

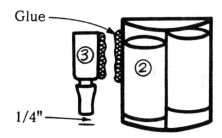

Important: Position the motor so there's 1/4" between the bottom of the rubber hosing and the bottom of the battery pack.

3. Connect Wires

Follow the simple wiring diagram below.

① On-Off Switch
SOLDER
–
+
RED
BLACK
RED
② Battery Pack
Motor ③


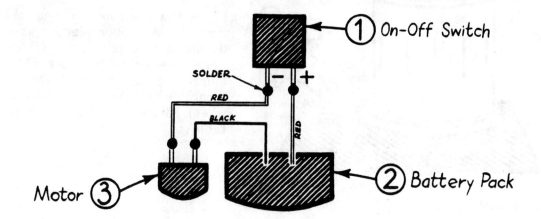

Use a fine tip (pencil) soldering iron and rosin core solder. If you don't have access to a soldering iron, some Radio Shack stores may be willing to loan you one. Or, if you don't want to solder, you can use crimp connectors--also available at Radio Shack.

Before you solder wires, touch them to the appropriate terminal (connecting points) to make sure the drive wheel (3A) is turning clockwise. If you're not sure which way it's rotating, place it against the zoetrope turntable (4)--the zoetrope should spin counterclockwise. Now you're ready to:

A. Solder the black battery pack wire to the motor.

B. Cut the red battery pack wire in half. Join the half that is connected to the battery pack to the positive terminal of the switch. (See diagram above.)

C. Solder the loose piece of red wire as follows: one end to the motor and the other end to the negative (-) terminal of the on/off switch. (See diagram above.)

4. Optional: Glue switch to the back of the battery pack. See diagram below. This will help prevent solder connections from breaking during use.

Switch
ON
OFF
Back of
Battery Pack


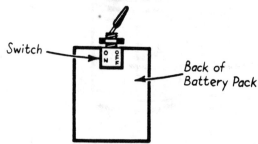

5. Happy Motoring!

# THE DELUXE ZOETROPE MOTOR

This deluxe "beauty" was also designed by Jim Samuels--and once again, all the parts (except the hosing) are available from Radio Shack. It's only a few dollars more than the "simple" motor and offers these features:

--a switch that gives you the choice of clockwise or counterclockwise rotation.

--a potentiometer for variable speeds.

--a compact plastic case to house all the parts and to protect all the soldered connections.

1. The Motor

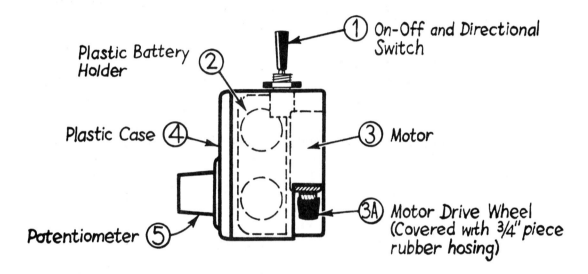

① On-Off and Directional Switch
Plastic Battery Holder ②
Plastic Case ④
③ Motor
3A Motor Drive Wheel (Covered with 3/4" piece rubber hosing)
Potentiometer ⑤


2. How It Works

①
②
③
④


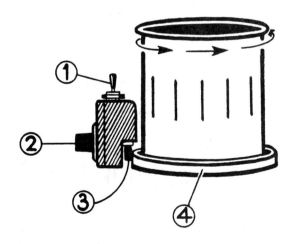

Place the zoetrope on a nonskid surface. Switch motor (1) on (select either clockwise or counterclockwise motion). Push the rotating rubber tube (3) against the side of the turntable (4). Regulate the speed at which the turntable moves by rotating the potentiometer knob (2).

3. Parts

Parts (1)-(5) are from Radio Shack; R.S. catalogue numbers are in parenthesis.

(1) DPDT (Double pole/double throw) toggle switch (#275-1545)

(2) Plastic Battery Holder and 2 "C" batteries (#270-385)

(3) DC (Direct Current) motor (#273-222)

(3A) Rubber Hosing (See simple Motor--Parts, p. 103)

(4) Deluxe Project Case (#270-222)

(5) Potentiometer 2.2K or 5K (#271-1714)
and knob: 1 3/8" diameter (#274-406)

4. Assembly

A. Place rubber hosing (3A) over motor drive wheel (3). See p. 103.

B. Follow the wiring diagram on p. 107. Use pencil soldering iron and rosin core solder. After connecting wires, turn power on to make sure all the parts are working.

C. Use a hack saw to cut opening for the drive wheel in plastic case (4). Follow the specifications below.

Case Cover
& Screws
7/16"
Cut Away
1 5/8"
1"
1"
Side View
Back View

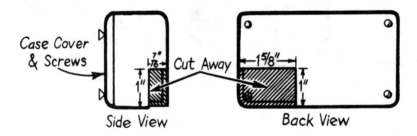

D. Drill holes for the on/off switch and the potentiometer in plastic case at points indicated by diagrams a) and b) below. Make sure the holes are slightly larger than the diameter of the potentiometer and switch shafts.

Case Cover
1"
5/8"
Cut Away

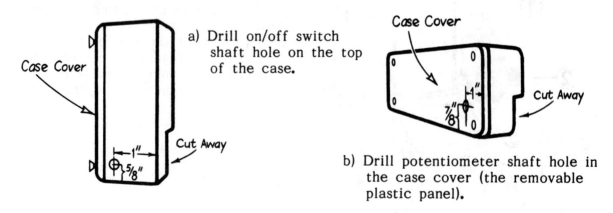

a) Drill on/off switch shaft hole on the top of the case.

Case Cover
1"
7/8"
Cut Away

b) Drill potentiometer shaft hole in the case cover (the removable plastic panel).

Deluxe Zoetrope Motor Wiring Diagram

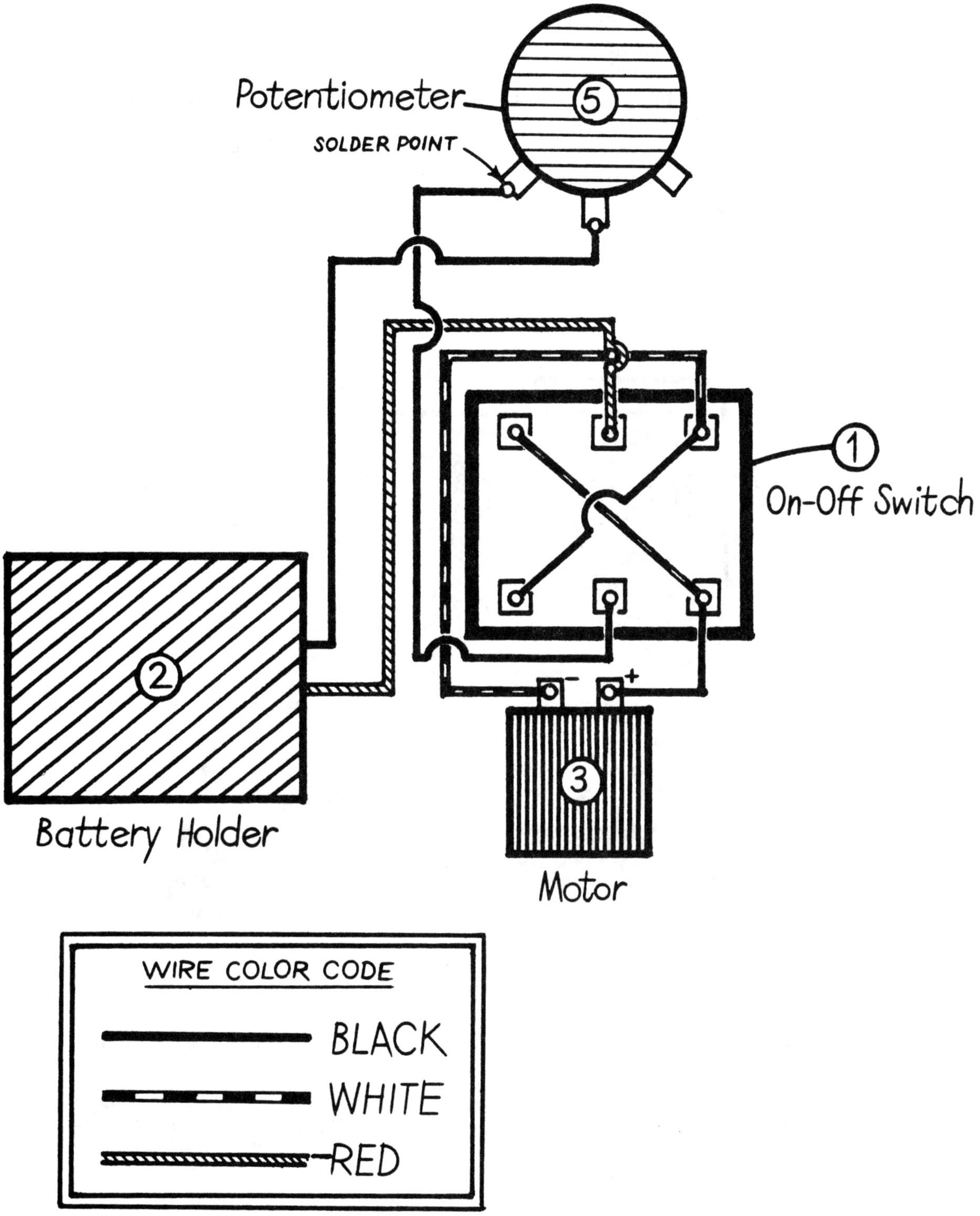

Potentiometer
5
SOLDER POINT
1
On-Off Switch
2
Battery Holder
-
+
3
Motor
WIRE COLOR CODE
BLACK
WHITE
RED

5. House all the motor parts (1), (2), (3) and (5) in plastic case (4). Follow these steps:

A. Remove plastic case cover and glue the motor (3) to the rear-right wall of the case. (Use Barge cement or any super glue.) Make sure the motor drive wheel rubber hosing is visible in the cut away portion of the plastic case. Position the motor so that the bottom of the rubber hosing is 5/8" from the bottom of the case. Trim hosing, if necessary. (See diagram at the right.)

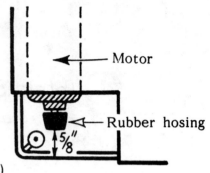

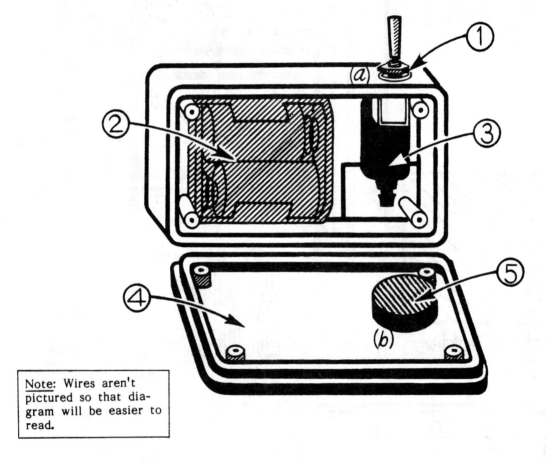

Note: Wires aren't pictured so that diagram will be easier to read.

B. Insert On/Off Switch (1) through drill hole (a) and tighten nut to hold it in place. See diagram above.

C. Glue Battery Pack (2) in place in the rear left of the case. See diagram above.

D. Insert Potentiometer (5) through hole (b) in the cover of the Plastic Case (4) and tighten nut to hold it in place. See diagram above and on the next page.

108

E. Close up Plastic Case by tightening the four screws in the case cover.

F. Cut the Potentiometer shaft with a hack saw so that it's 1/2" to 5/8" long. See diagram below-left.

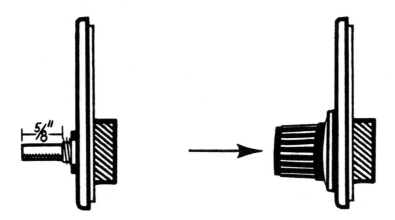

Potentiometer (5) and Plastic Case Cover - Side view

G. Mount knob on the Potentiometer shaft and tighten the knob screw. See diagram above-right.

H. Congratulations. You are now a Deluxe Zoetrope Motorist!

# How to Build a Light Table

A light table is <u>not</u> an essential tool for successful zoetroping. It's a luxury item, a luxury you just might want to give yourself (or your students). With simple tools you can slap one together in a few hours.

The purpose of the light table is simple: it will enable you to trace any line, shape or image quickly and accurately. Use the light table for tracing frame lines, spacing guides, reference lines or any image that's going to repeat unchanged frame after frame.

Since there's no absolutely right way to build a light table, the directions that follow are somewhat cursory. Change the dimensions and materials to suit your needs and pocketbook. And remember: it doesn't have to be beautiful, it just has to work.

<u>Suggested Materials</u>

--1/2" Plywood

Use it for the top, bottom and sides of the light table. It can be painted, stained or left unfinished.

--18" or 24" Fluorescent Fixture

Fluorescent tubes burn much cooler than incandesent bulbs and will light your drawing area more evenly.

--In-Line Switch (15 amp)

An easy to install on/off switch.

--16 Gage Lamp Cord and Wall Socket Plug

--10" x 12" "Lighting White"

Use it for the illuminated drawing area. You should be able to find this inexpensive, milky, translucent acrylic at most retail plastic stores.

<u>Suggested Dimensions</u>

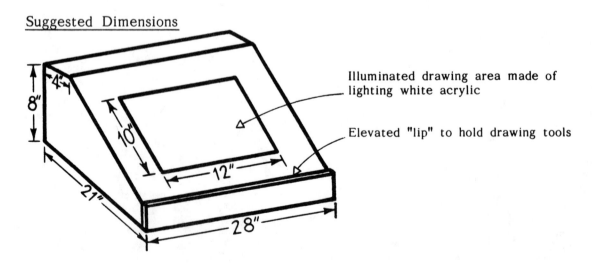

Illuminated drawing area made of lighting white acrylic

Elevated "lip" to hold drawing tools

SIDE

Fluorescent light fixture placed under plastic for maximum illumination Make sure "lighting white" is flush with the surface of the light table.

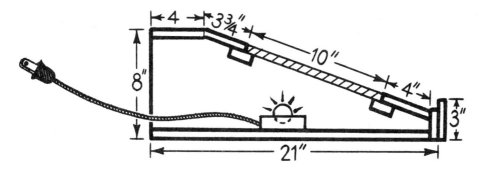

REAR

Back of the light table can remain open. Insert In-line switch in the 16 gauge lamp cord for easy on and off.

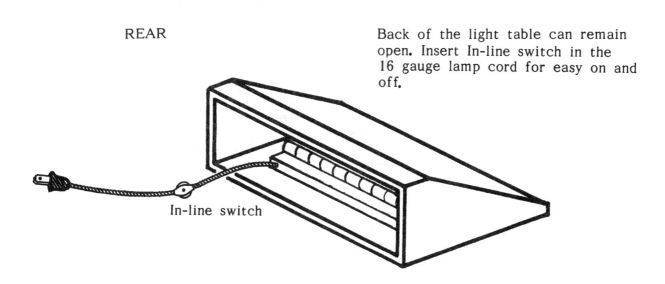

In-line switch

# Books

Animation by Preston Blair, Walter Foster Art Books, Tustin, California.
Paperback: $2.95

For anyone interested in cartoon animation, this book is a must. Blair,
an old-time Disney animator, explains everything from character design
to the basic laws of motion in language that anyone can easily understand. The book's cheap price makes it one of the world's last bar-
gains.

The Animation Book by Kit Laybourne, Crown, NY, NY, 1979. Paperback: $10.95

If you want to move on to other forms of animation, this book will
help you get started. Author Laybourne discusses the tools of the trade
(cameras, film, lighting) and demystifies many animation techniques
including stop motion, pixillation, sand, clay, cut-outs, line and cel.
Lavishly illustrated.

Animals in Motion by Edweard Muybridge, Dover Publications, Inc., NY, NY.
Hardcover: $15.95

This monumental photographic work, produced at the University of Pennsylvania between 1884-85, contains detailed motion sequences of scores
of animals from horses to gnus. It remains the indispensable guide for
anyone wanting to do (or teach) animation involving animal locomotion.
A companion text, "The Human Figure in Motion" is also published by
Dover.

Paper Movie Machines by Bud Wentz, Troubador Press, San Francisco, 1975.
Paperback: $3.95

This fun, inexpensive book invites you to assemble nearly a dozen persistence of vision toys (all relatives of the zoetrope) using the simple cut outs included in the book. Like The Zoetrope Book, Paper
Movie Machines encourages free wheeling creativity on a shoestring.

Perspective Drawing by Ernest Norling, Walter Foster Art Books, Tustin,
California. Paperback: $2.95

For folks interested in spatial animation this book will help you get
a handle on various ways to represent the third dimension on paper.
Author Norling deals with everything you'll ever need to know (vanish-
ing points, horizon lines, one, two and three point perspective...).
The diagrams are pretty easy to follow and the language is friendly.

112

# ABOUT THE AUTHOR

Originally a painter, Roger Kukes received his B.F.A. from Wayne State University and his M.F.A. from Yale University. He began making films in New York City with a borrowed 8mm movie camera in the late 1960's. Since 1976, Kukes' award winning experimental and animated films have been seen at festivals world wide including The New York Film Festival, Film Ex (Los Angeles) and the Annecy (France) International Animated Film Festival.

Also an energetic lecturer and teacher, Kukes is dedicated to "encouraging and empowering everyone's precious creative potential". He works in a variety of Artists in Education programs around the Pacific Northwest, and has led scores of drawing and animation workshops at schools, colleges, film centers and museums from Los Angeles to Seattle.

While a member of The Animation Collective, Kukes helped to produce The First International Zoetrope Competition (1979). He is the creator of Flowering, a 56 page flipbook, published by Metropolis Graphics (N.Y., N.Y., 1981), and recently received a Western States Arts Foundation Fellowship for animation.

Kukes lives in Portland, Oregon with his wife Linnea and two brown-eyed daughters, Maya and Norah.

## Have Zoetrope: Will Travel

Roger Kukes will visit your school, university, film center or museum. A variety of workshops and large group presentations are available. Contact Roger at Klassroom Kinetics--3758 SE Taylor Street, Portland, OR 97214. Or call (503) 235-0933.

# GLOSSARY

ABRUPT STRIP    A non-cyclical zoetrope strip that changes progressively across all 12 frames. Since frames #1 and #12 are very different, one sudden (or "abrupt") change is noticed when viewing.

BARGE CEMENT    One of the best glues for affixing zoetropes to (Rubbermaid) turntables. Available from Birkenstock shoe stores, or from your local cobbler.

THE BIG FIVE    1) Ideas 2) Images 3) Progressive Change 4) Motion 5) Message

BLACK LIGHT    Used in a darkened room, this near ultra violet light gives fluorescent colors a weirdly beautiful incandescence.

CLEAN UP    A "rough" that has had all inessential lines and shapes erased (see ROUGH).

CONTINUOUS ACTION STRIP    A cyclical zoetrope strip having no repeating frames.

CRAZY QUILT STRIP    Distinctly different images are created in each of the strip's 12 frames.

CYCLE    An action that repeats continuously. For the zoetroper, creating a cycle means designing a strip so that frame #12 leads logically back to frame #1.

ERASER    Animators/zoetropers often use this as frequently as they use the lead of a pencil.

EXAGGERATION    The essence of exaggeration is overstatement. It's the crucial element in animation with "ZIP". To the zoetroper, exaggerating often means designing frames #1 and #6 so that they are very different.

THE EXPERIMENTAL APPROACH    The free wheeling, no holds barred attitude that values playfulness, inquiry and risk above everything else. You may end up with a mess (or a masterpiece), but no matter. The real payoff for the experimenter is the process of testing and discovery.

FRAMELESS STRIP    Images are created across the strip without regard for framelines.

FORESHORTENING    A graphic trick designed to accentuate a three dimensional reading of a drawing or diagram. Specifically, lines are presented as shorter than they actually are so as to conform to the laws of perspective.

FRAME    One of the 12 image compartments found on the standard zoetrope strip.

FRAME LINES    The vertical lines that serve to separate one frame from another on the standard zoetrope strip.

HOLD    A perceivable pause that results when two or more identical (or nearly identical) frames are repeated.

IDEA PAPER    A preliminary sketch showing the basic plan for a strip as a series of progressively changing images. Great for brainstorming and for getting the creative juices flowing.

INBETWEEN    The increments or frames between the key images.

114

KEY IMAGE    One of the defining phases of a movement, it often comes at the beginning or the end of an animated sequence. In many zoetrope strips, frames #1 and #6 are the key images.

LATERAL MOTION    The movement of a shape or object across a zoetrope strip from right to left, or left to right.

METAMORPHOSIS (METAMORPHOSE)    To incrementally change one thing into another.

MOTION GAME PLAN    An animator's strategy (often expressed as a diagram with arrows) for moving a shape or object from one position to another.

MULTIPLE MOVEMENTS    When more than one graphic element is set in motion within a frame or across frame lines.

1-12, 6-7 STRIP    This is the easiest zoetrope strip to design. Frames #7-#12 are a mirror image of frames #1-#6. Also, there are two holds: one at frames #1 and #12, and the other at frames #6 and #7.

PERSISTENCE OF VISION    The physiological phenomenon enabling the human eye/brain to see a series of still pictures as apparently in motion. (See p. 11).

PROGRESSIVE CHANGE    The lifeblood of all animation including the zoetrope: ideas are expressed as a series of logically progessing image increments. The degree of the difference between the successive image increments greatly affects the quality of the motion we see.

REFERENCE LINES    Lightly drawn pencil lines of any sort (horizontals, verticals, diagonals) that help the zoetroper position shapes accurately from frame to frame.

ROUGH    An animator's drawing that is full of searching, tentative lines, yet finally succeeds in locating and defining shapes.

SHORT ZOETROPE    A trimmed down version of the standard (3 gallon ice cream drum) zoetrope. This is the preferred zoetrope for kids (and many adults) because it's easier to insert and remove strips. (See p. 98).

SPACING GUIDE    A diagram that helps the animator work out a series of progressive changes, and a smooth path of motion.

SPATIAL ANIMATION    The presentation of images on a flat surface so that they appear to move in the third dimension.

SPEED LINES    Usually a series of parallel lines that follow behind an object and trace its path of motion. Used to suggest very rapid motion.

# AVAILABLE FROM KLASSROOM KINETICS

**The Zoetrope Book**          $14.95 each
>   Includes 9 original zoetrope strips which can be viewed in your Zoetrope

**Zoetropes**          $55.00 each
>   A rugged ready to use black, 3 gallon ice cream drum zoetrope
>   mounted on a 10 1/2" Rubbermaid turntable.

**Sample Zoetrope Strips**          $10.50 a set
>   A set includes these six new Zoetrope Strips

>   --   Star Eater

>   --   Bell Ringer

>   --   Smoke Stacks

>   --   Heart/Shadows

>   --   Boat and Waves

>   --   Metamorphosis:  Horse into Moon

## Order Form

**The Zoetrope Book**

>   Number of Copies _____ x $14.95 ea.          _____

**Zoetropes**

>   Number of Zoetropes _____ x $55.00 ea.          _____

**Sample Strips**

>   Number of Sets _____ x $10.50 ea.          _____

>                                         Sub Total     _____

Shipping/Handling

>   Please add $2.00 for the first item ordered

>   and $1.50 for <u>EACH</u> additional item          _____


>                                         TOTAL          _____

Name _____

Address _____

City _____ State _____ Zip _____

**KLASSROOM KINETICS          3758 S.E. Taylor     Portland, OR     97214**

# Sample Strips

On the following pages you'll find five sample zoetrope strips for viewing in your zoetrope.

1. Cut out the three strip sections A, B and C on each page. Join the sections together using masking tape. Make sure that there aren't any gaps between the sections when you tape them together.

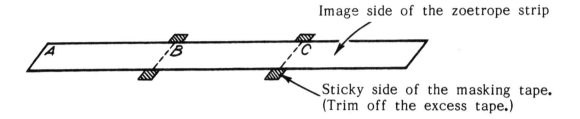

Image side of the zoetrope strip

Sticky side of the masking tape. (Trim off the excess tape.)

2. Here's what the completed strip should look like.

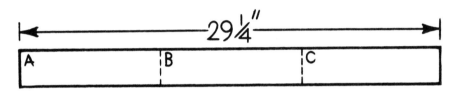

$29\frac{1}{4}''$

The Master strip on p. 131 can be used as a guide for drawing frame lines on blank strips.

The Lateral Motion Guide on p. 133 will enable you to locate the positions for 10's, 11's and 13's. (See also Lateral Motion, p. 58).

> IMPORTANT: When removing strips from the book, cut along the black line near the binding with an X-acto knife. Do not tear pages out or the binding of the book will be weakened.

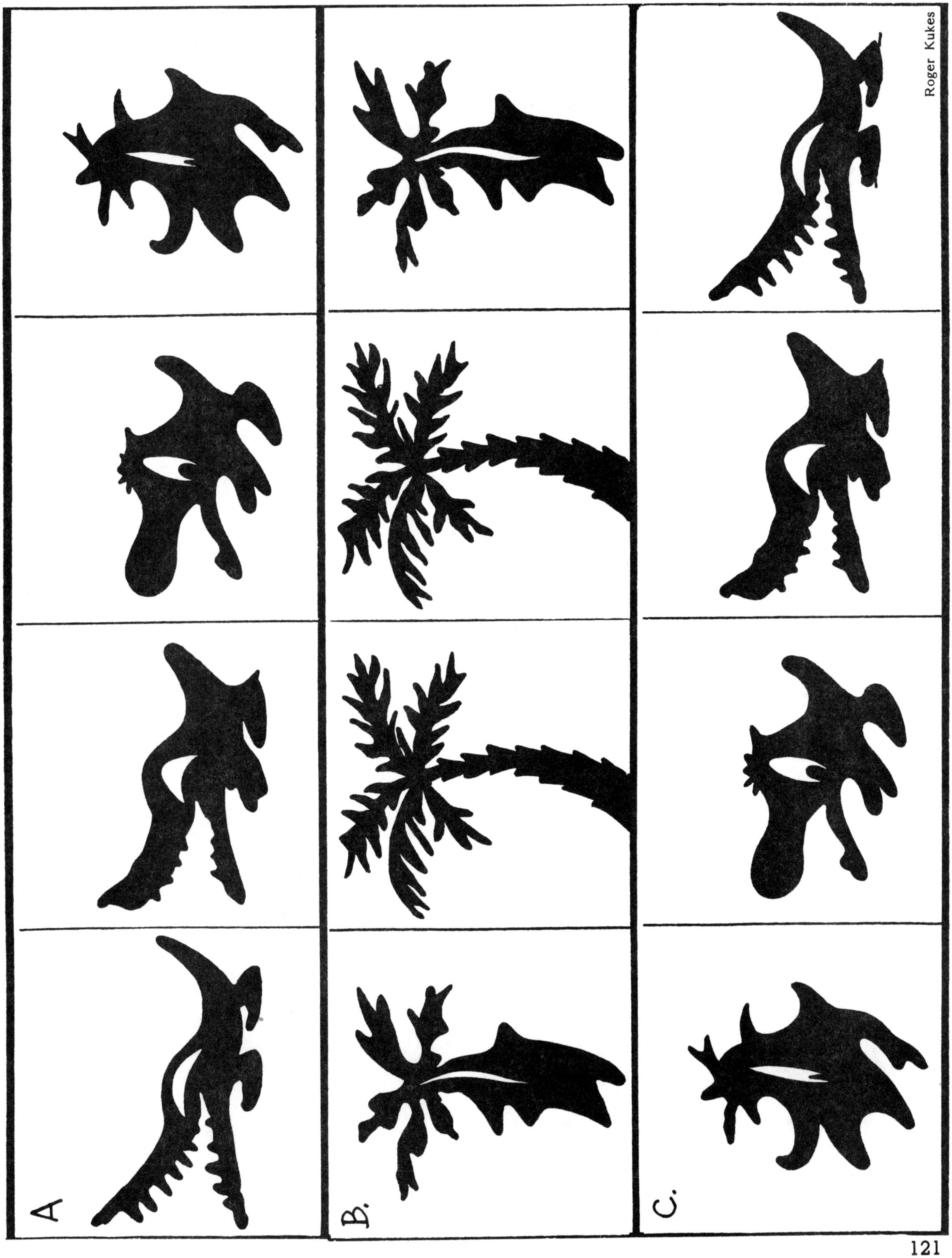
A
B.
C.
Roger Kukes

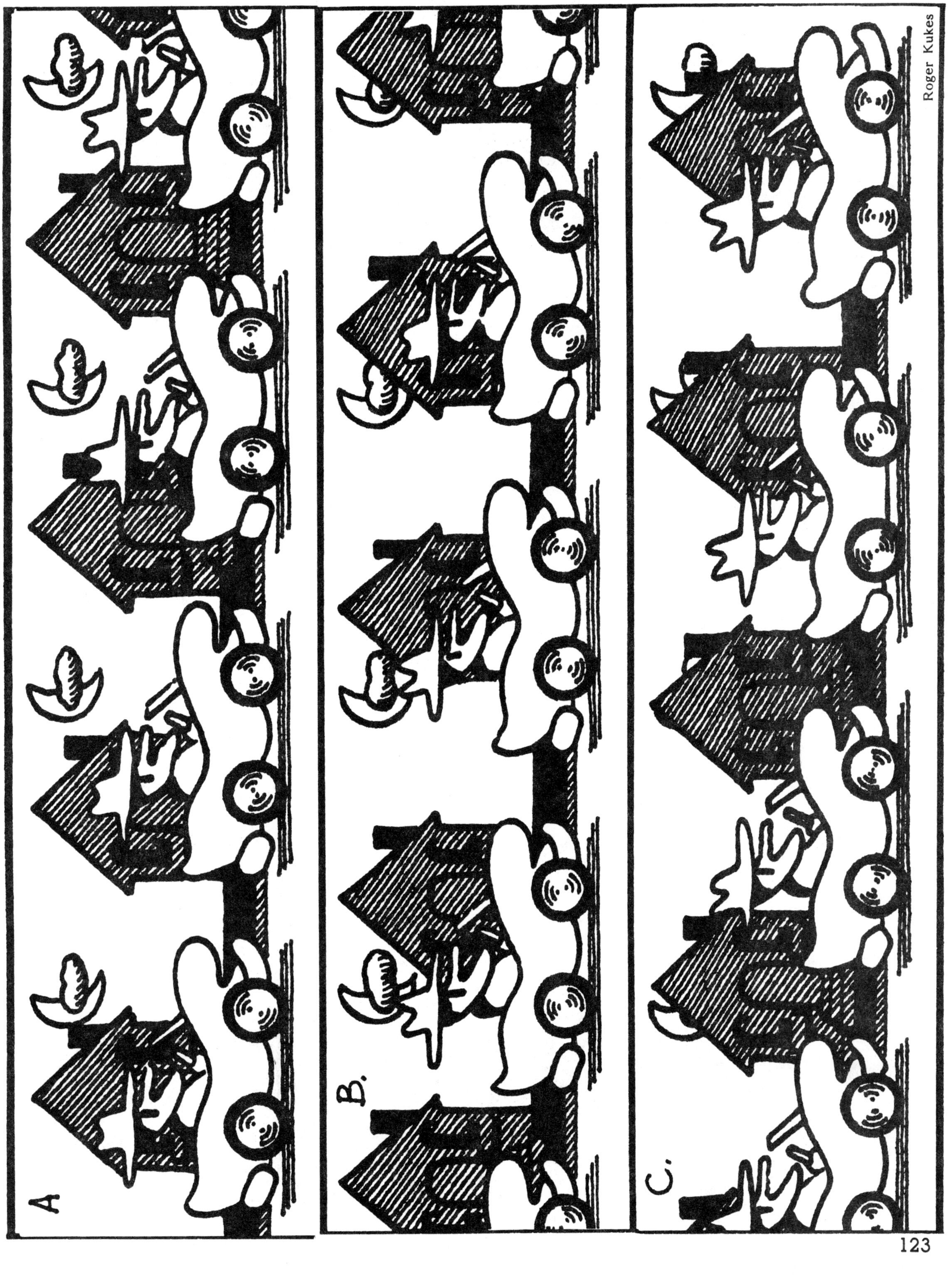
A
B.
C.
Roger Kukes

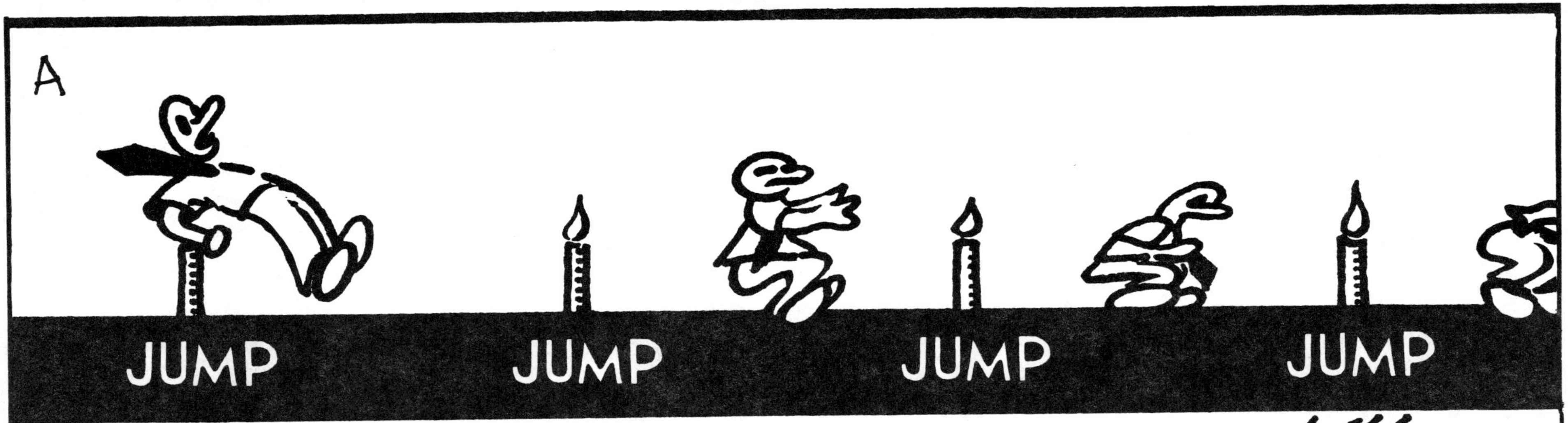
A
JUMP
JUMP
JUMP
JUMP

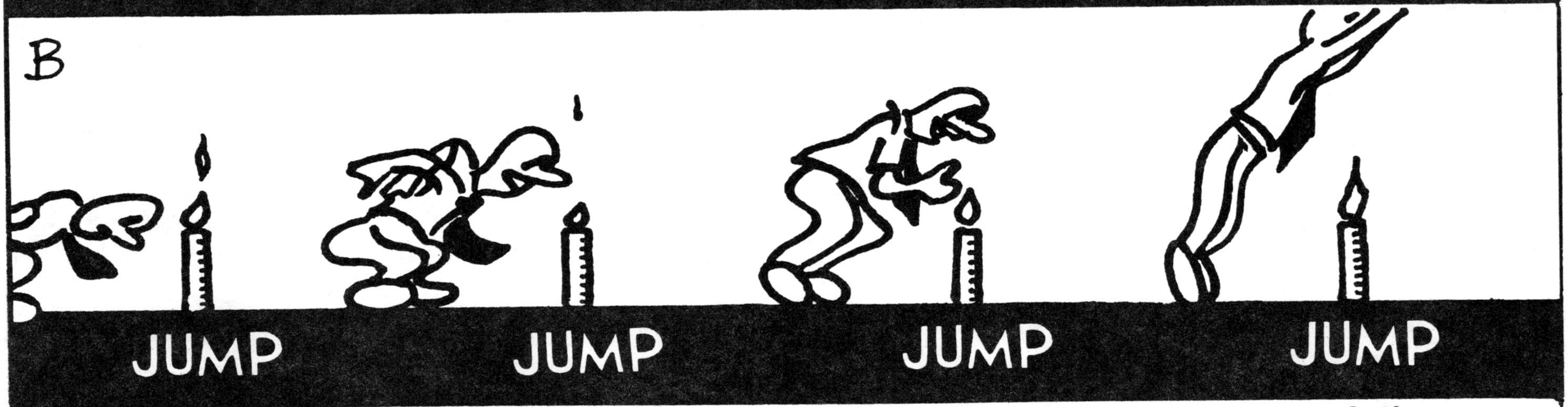
B
JUMP
JUMP
JUMP
JUMP

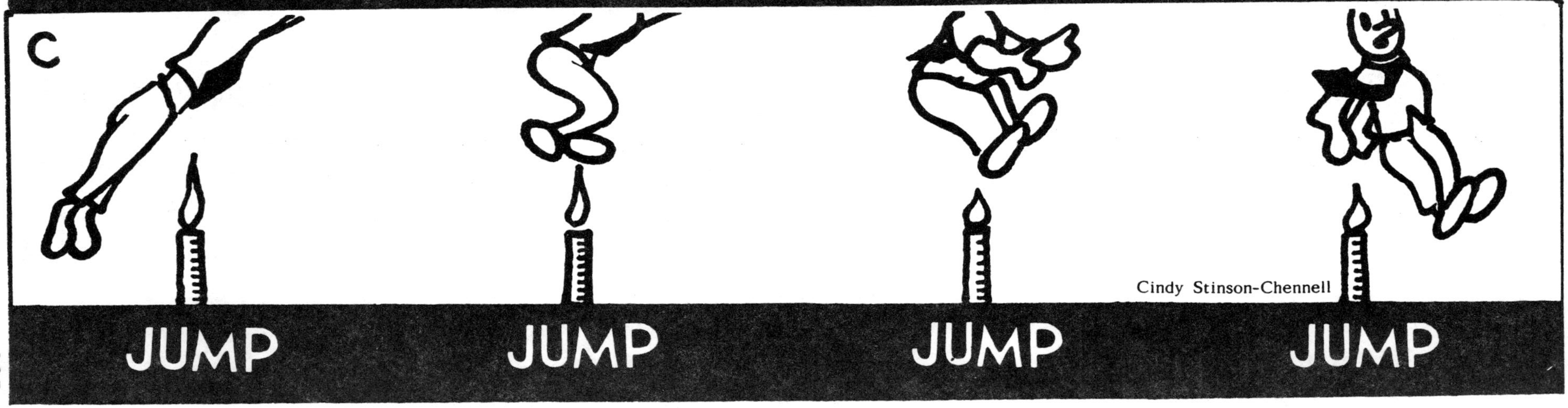
C
JUMP
JUMP
JUMP
JUMP
Cindy Stinson-Chennell

126

© CINDY STINSON-CHENNELL-1985

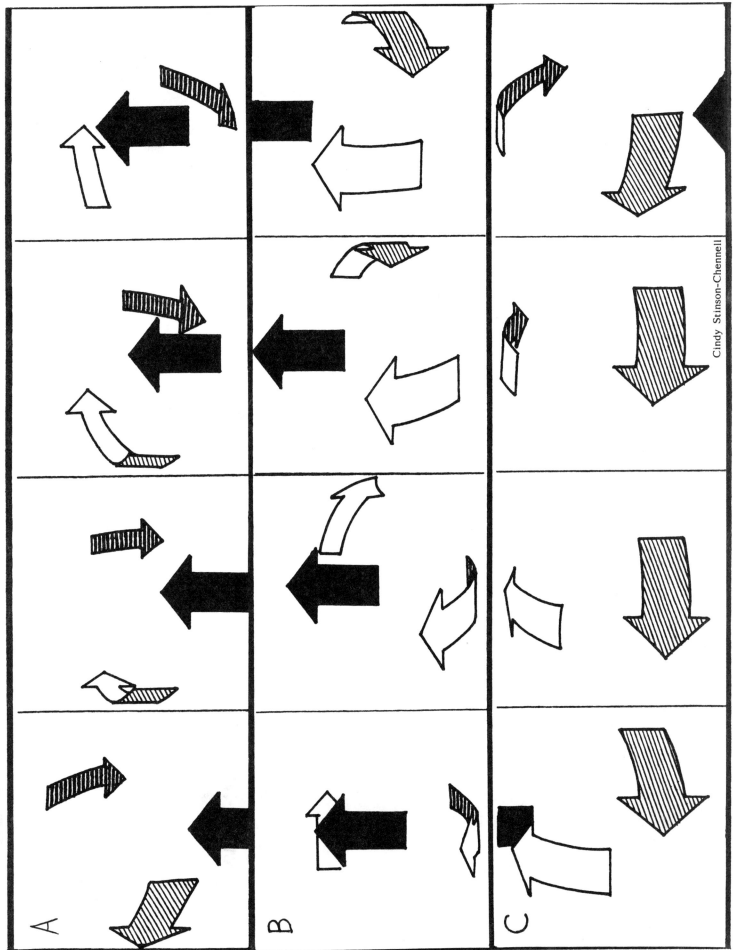

Cindy Stinson-Chennell

128

© CINDY STINSON-CHENNELL-1985

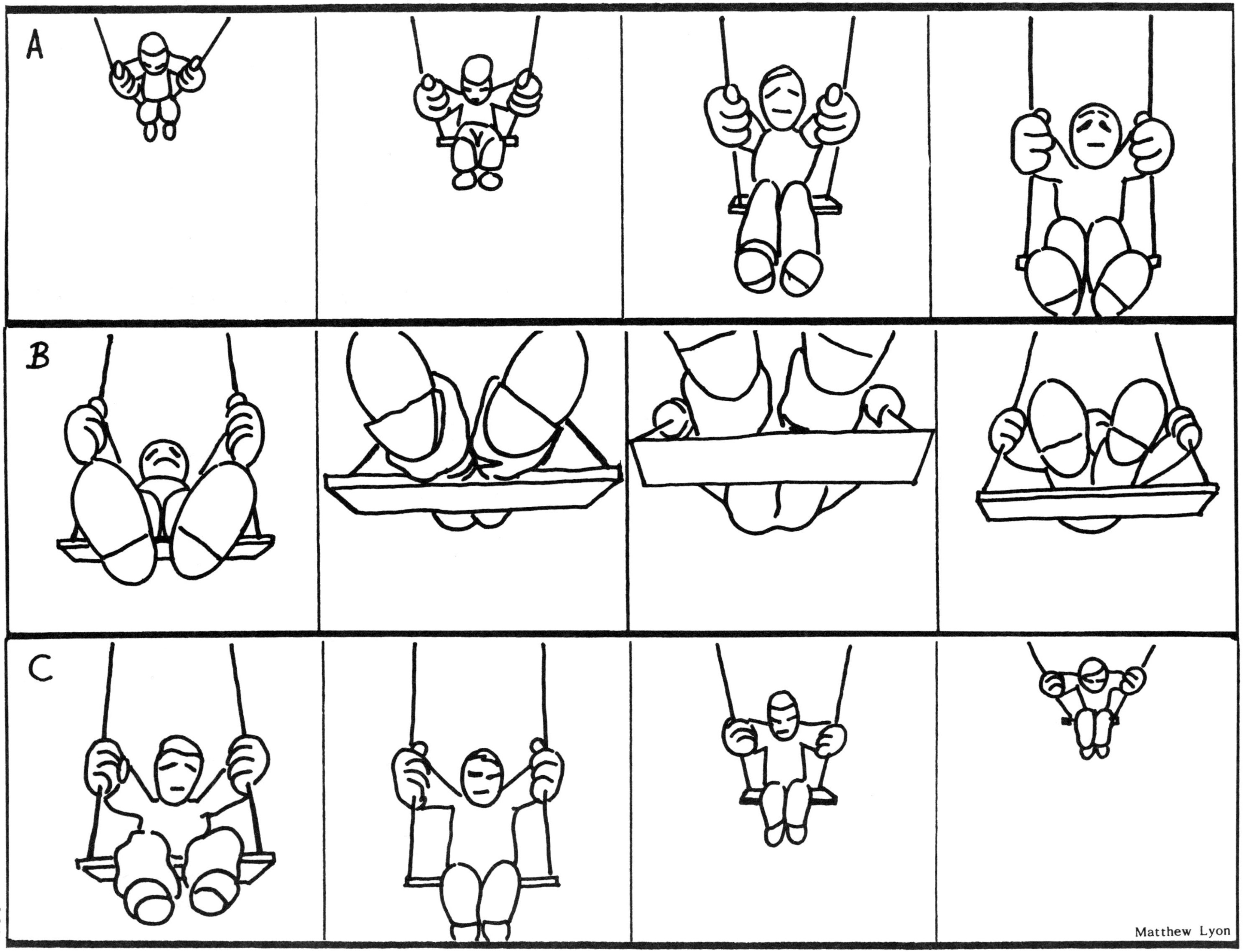
A
B
C
Matthew Lyon

A.

B.

C.

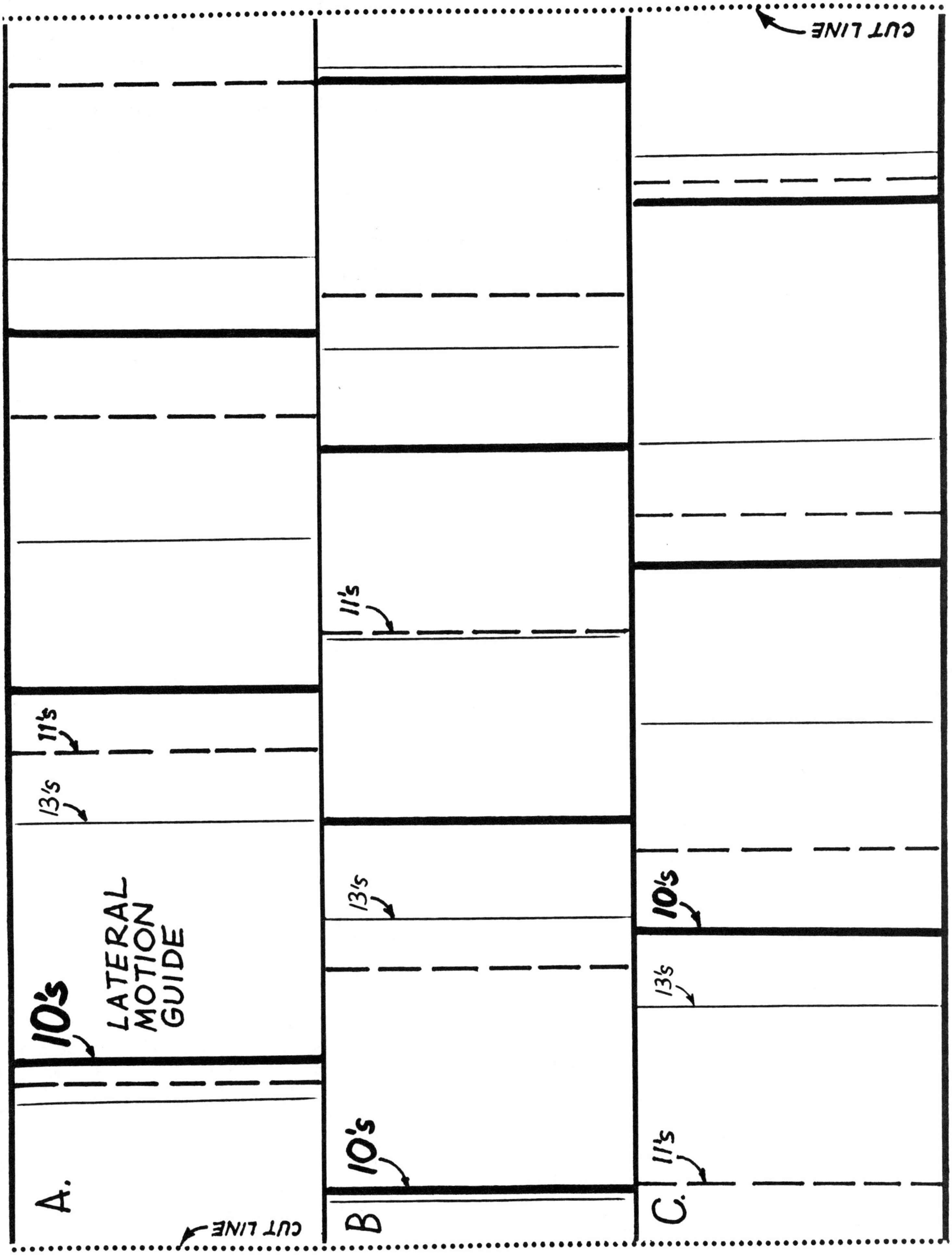
LATERAL MOTION GUIDE
A.
B.
C.
10's
11's
13's
CUT LINE

134

© KLASSROOM KINETICS 1985

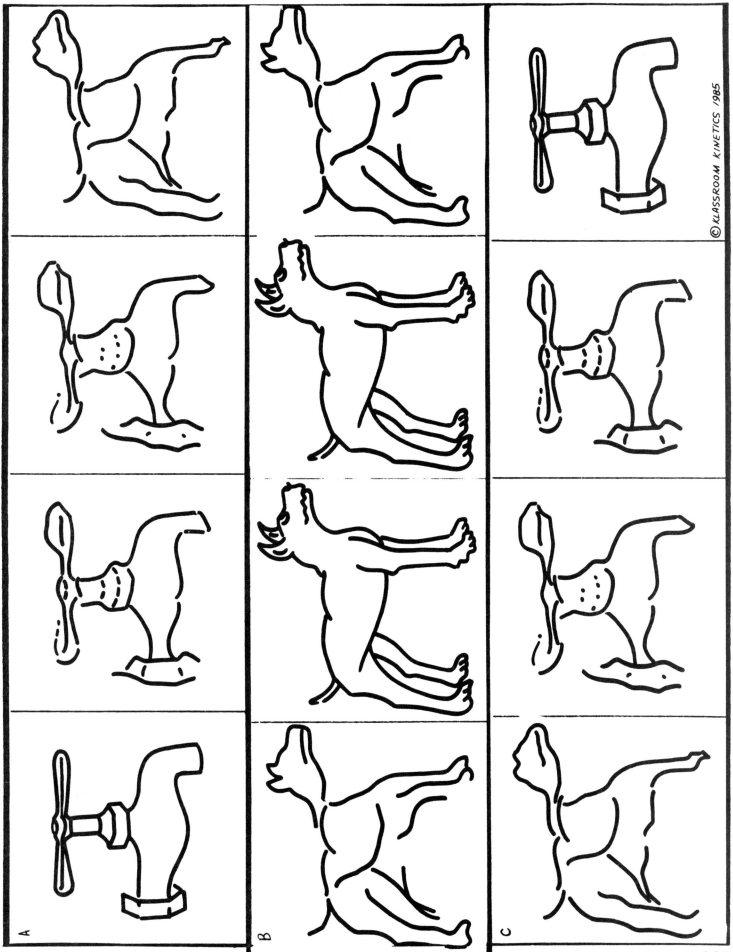

A

B

C

135

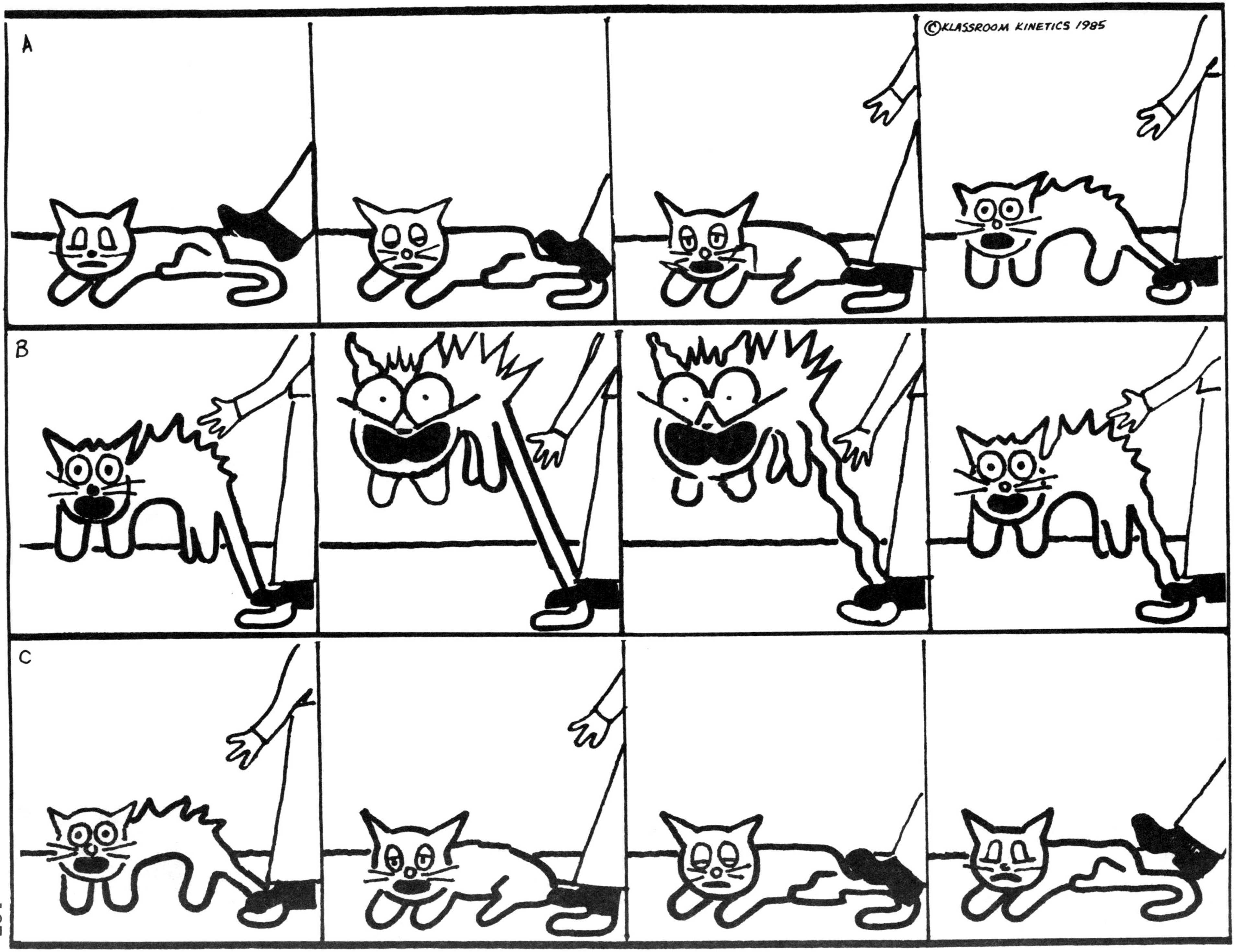
A
©KLASSROOM KINETICS 1985
B
C

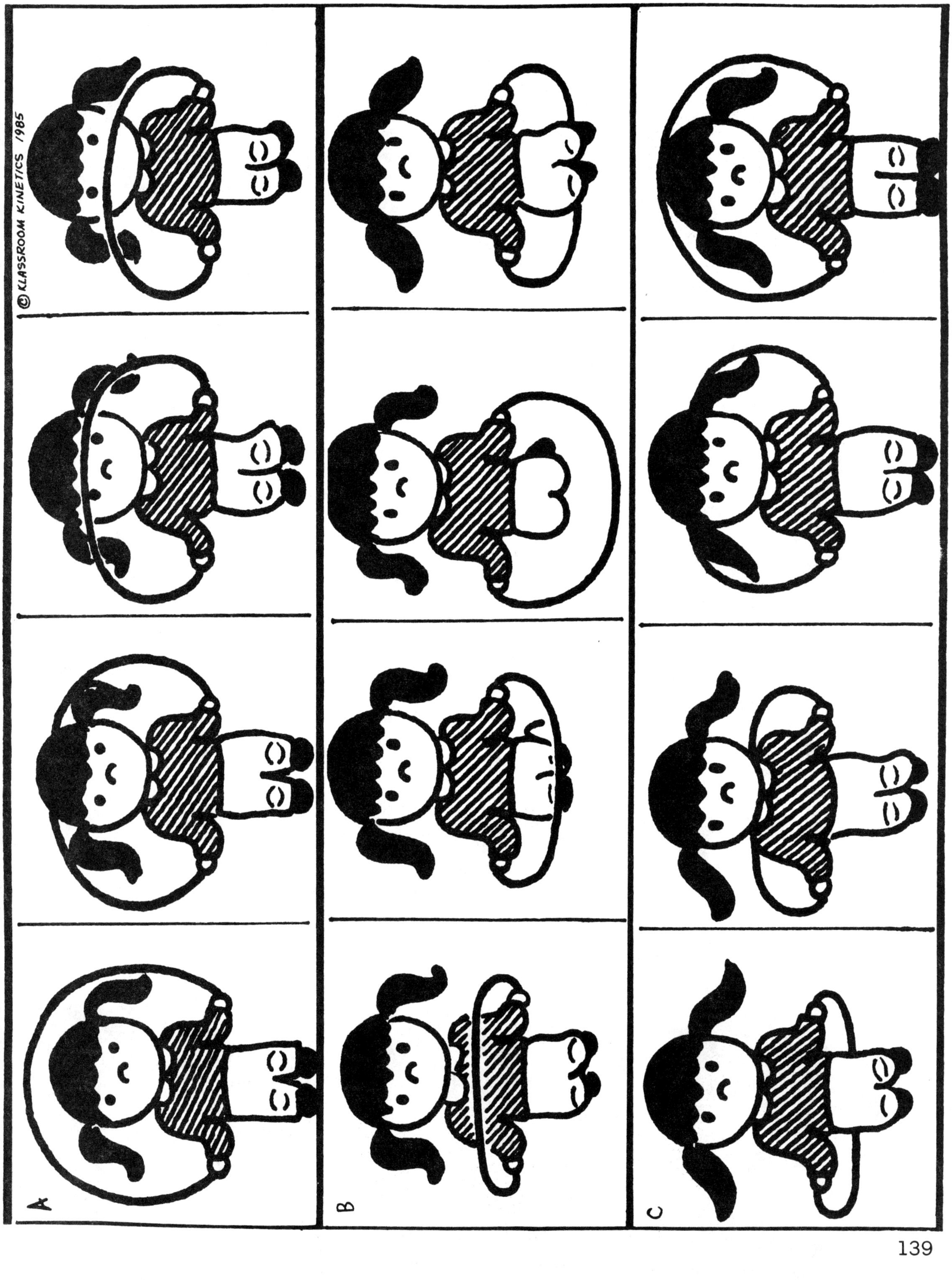
© KLASSROOM KINETICS 1985
A
B
C

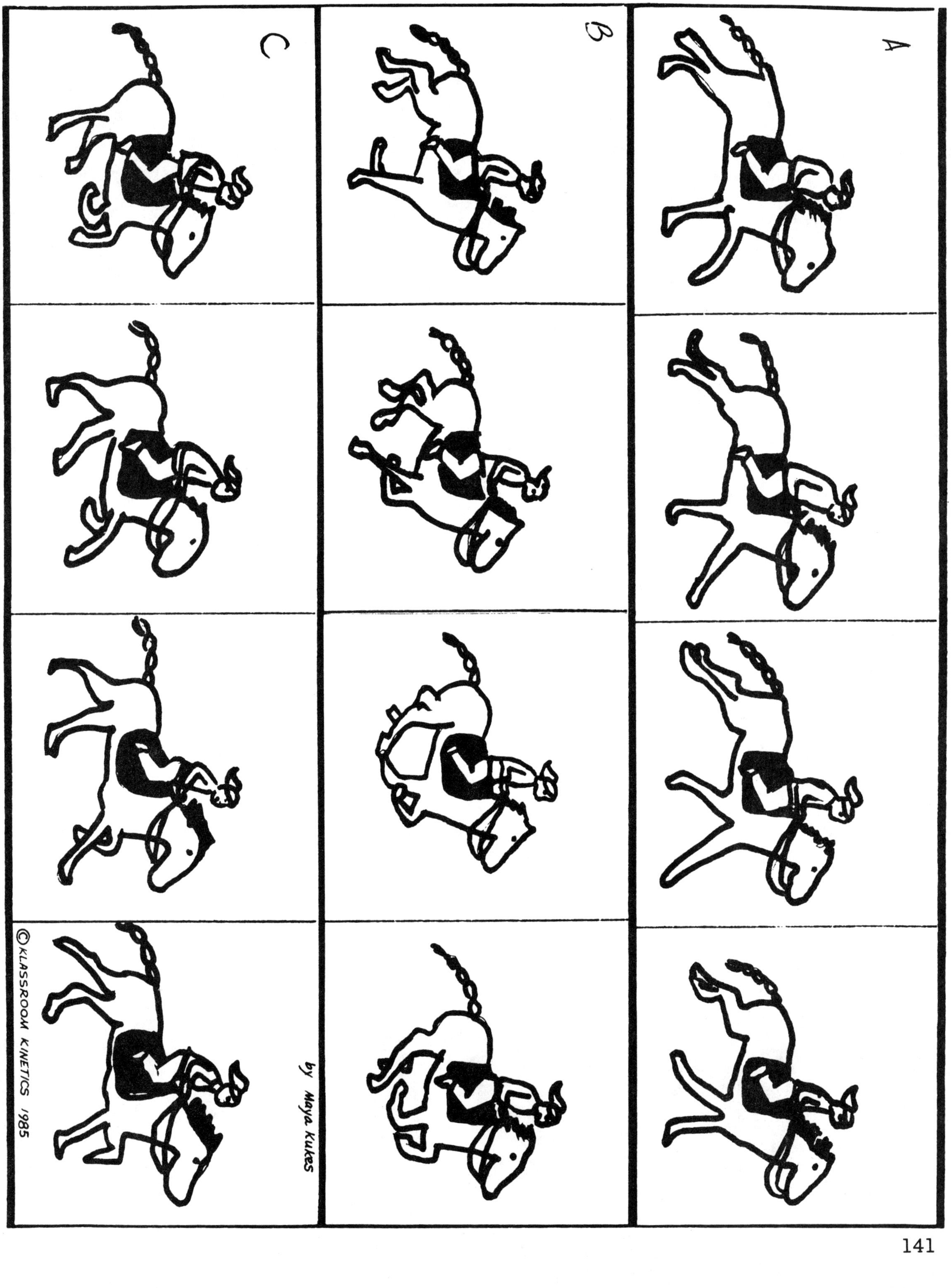
A
B
C
by Maya Kukes
© KLASSROOM KINETICS 1985

142